SPINNING

for Fresh Water *Game Fish*

By Joseph D. Bates, Jr.

SPINNING FOR AMERICAN GAME FISH

TROUT WATERS AND HOW TO FISH THEM

STREAMER FLY FISHING IN FRESH AND SALT WATER

SPINNING FOR FRESH WATER GAME FISH

From a Painting by Jack Murray

SPINNING

for Fresh Water *Game Fish*

By JOSEPH D. BATES, Jr.

Illustrated with drawings
by
JACK MURRAY
and with photographs

Little, Brown and Company · Boston · Toronto

Published simultaneously in Canada
by Little, Brown & Company (Canada) Limited

PRINTED IN THE UNITED STATES OF AMERICA

To

GASTON ROGER MIEG

A SPORTSMAN AND A FRIEND

Foreword

BY H. G. TAPPLY

Associate Editor of FIELD & STREAM MAGAZINE; *author of* THE FLY TYER'S HANDBOOK *and* TACKLE TINKERING

IT ALWAYS is a considerable event when Joe Bates writes a book, because each of his first three have pioneered in relatively unexplored fields of angling. His first one, *Spinning for American Game Fish,* introduced and described this then new fishing method to America and undoubtedly was a dominant influence in the present widespread acceptance of the sport.

His second gave a detailed account of where trout of the various species are to be found under changing climatic conditions and how to catch them under these circumstances. Just after he wrote the book, Joe and another well-known angler went fishing at Lake Pend Oreille, Idaho. It seems that on the first two days there they both failed to catch one of the lake's big Kamloops rainbow trout. The other angler quite logically complained to Joe that he should know where the fish were because he had just written a book about it.

Nettled by this rebuke, Joe explored his mind for data and then they both went to a spot on the big lake where he suggested. To make a long story short: inside of an hour or so, Joe hooked and landed the record rainbow trout of the year — a thirty-one-pound, twelve-ounce monster that was a close contender for the world's record, and that still is the largest rainbow trout ever taken on light tackle. He took the fish by the spinning method, of course — with a rod he himself had designed. Since then, his *Trout Waters and How to Fish Them* has become somewhat of a classic in angling literature.

Next, Joe produced *Streamer Fly-Fishing in Fresh and Salt Water*, a most fascinating work telling how to select and use these streamer flies, which imitate baitfish rather than insects. He has collected patterns of hundreds of streamers and bucktails, as dressed by their originators, and he gives authentic and detailed instructions for tying more than two hundred and fifty of the most prominent of them.

Now, he's back again to his first love of spinning, and what he has to say will make the subject easier, more productive and more fun for everybody.

It is quite proper that Joe should follow up his first book with this new one. He has written more magazine articles on spinning than any other person in America, and he is so well known in this field that he frequently is referred to as "Mr. Spinning" himself. His knowledge of spinning is international, rather than merely sectional. He has used rods and lures of his design on both fresh and salt waters from the Canadian wilderness to the Florida Keys; from the coast of Maine to the steelhead rivers of the West. With this tackle he has taken many notable fish. His travels have taken him to Europe, to Australia, and to many other far-flung regions. He is a sought-after consultant for several major tackle firms, even though his vocation is that of an advertising-agency executive.

Those of us who also write about fishing consider Joe one of America's most practical anglers. He gives his readers all the information they need without cluttering their minds with unnecessary technical details or extraneous material. He leavens his instructions with colorful anecdotes of actual fishing, not only telling his readers exactly how to get greatest enjoyment from the sport but also making them feel that they are his companions on the trip.

Nowadays there is a tremendous diversity of reels, rods, lines and lures from which spinning anglers may choose. Some are excellent; some leave room for improvement, and some which are sold as spinning equipment are not such at all. In this book, Joe tells how to separate the wheat from the chaff. He explains the requirements of suitable tackle and he gives authoritative reasons for his observations. This should safeguard his readers from making unwise investments in tackle and should contribute immeasurably to their fun and to their success.

Then, Joe goes on to explain how to select and mate
the elements of the various strengths of tackle used in
fresh water spinning, because he correctly believes
that properly matched tackle is vitally important to
success. He explains why a few sensibly selected lures
are better than an indiscriminate collection of many,
and which types and sizes to use for the various kinds
of fishing. He tells how to rig tackle for most favorable
use under all conditions and he gives fishermen many
new ideas that are sure to improve their sport.

How to select and assemble the tackle is of vital
importance, but how to use it properly is even more so.
Here, Joe's experience and his ability to write about it
provide his readers with instruction almost impossible for them to acquire by themselves. After reading
this book, I am sure that no angler can go spinning for
any type of fresh water game fish in any kind of water
and not know how to do it intelligently and with maximum success. Those of us who have had difficulties
using spinning tackle will learn in this book how such
troubles quickly and easily can be avoided. Those of
us who understand spinning fairly well will find herein
many new suggestions sure to contribute to more favorable results.

Joe is not one of those biased fishermen who consider spinning the answer to all angling problems. He
frankly discusses its limitations as well as its advantages. When we go fishing together, he always takes a
spinning rod, but he takes a fly rod as well; using ei-

ther the one or the other, as conditions seem to dictate.
Thus, this book will prove an authoritative and
practical mine of information for those who think they
might enjoy spinning, as well as for old hands at the
game. But, in commending it to its readers, I should
voice a word of warning. If you don't want to go spinning, put the book down now. If you read it, it is almost certain that you'll be a spinning addict hence-
forth!

H. G. TAPPLY

Lexington, Massachusetts

Contents

Illustrations, Maps and Charts

Introduction

WHEN THE SPORT of spinning was so new in America that none of the tackle was made here and almost none had been imported from abroad, I chanced on a portentous day to be trying my fly rod on a western Massachusetts trout river. The leaves of the new year still slumbered in their tiny buds, and glistening patches of snow hid from the sun beneath fragrant evergreens and entangled laurel. The sweet, damp smell of spring was in the air and the spirits of anglers were high, because this was the warm and sunny afternoon of the opening day of our trout fishing season.

In this section, the river was so wide that no fly rod fisherman standing on one bank could drop his fly close to the other. Melting snows along mountain tributaries caused the waters to run deep and fast; too cold and discolored for good fly-fishing. Even my favorite streamers and bucktails, always a bulwark of the early season, had elicited little interest from the trout.

Slow progress over and around the giant boulders bordering the river brought me to a brook mouth which often had produced good fishing, even this early in the season. But the brook was across the river, and the river was far too deep and turbulent to wade. My longest casts having fallen far short of their mark, I sat on a rock to light my pipe and to study the water.

While I was resting, another angler approached. He carried no fly-fishing tackle but, instead, a slightly shorter and stiffer rod equipped with surprisingly large guides and a long cork grip. Affixed to the grip and standing well out from it hung an unusual reel whose spool faced toward the rod tip, rather than to the side. From the spool there issued a line identical in appearance and nearly so in size to the tippet of my fly-line leader. And from the line's end there dangled a very tiny spinner.

The fisherman sat down beside me to discuss our luck and to chat about the stream. In his creel, three large and beautiful brook trout lay upon a bed of moss. I asked about his tackle and he handed it to me to examine.

"Outfits like these are very popular in Europe," he said. "In England, the method is called 'thread-line' fishing, and in France, *lancer léger*, which means 'light casting.' Since the line uncoils from a fixed spool, rather than unrolling from a rotating one, the almost negligible friction makes possible longer, easier casts with lighter lines and lures. The adjustable brake acts as a slipping clutch which is set to give line automatically when need be, thus preventing a fish from breaking it. All this results in a very sporting and successful way to fish."

I asked the angler if he could reach the brook mouth and, at his nod, suggested that he try it.

He walked to the water and, with a single quick flip of his wrist, made the little lure soar out to land more than a hundred feet away close by a rock on the far side of the stream. On his third cast, he hooked and landed a large brook trout. Then he let me try the outfit, and eventually I caught one also.

Why was it relatively so easy for the spinning angler to take fish at a time when fly casters had no luck at all? As I look back upon the occurrence, the answer is obvious. The spinning angler could cover more water and he could cover it more quickly. His lures, being brighter, could be seen more readily in the high and murky stream. Of even greater importance, their weight caused them to sink deeper into the fast current, bringing them nearer to the fish, which were lying in the quiet water near the bottom. Since then, I have seen spinning anglers take fish when fly-fishermen could not do so under the same conditions — on trout streams in Colorado, on steelhead rivers in Oregon and northern California and in many other places. Thus, my introduction to spinning taught me one very pertinent reason for the popularity of the tackle. There are a great many others, as we shall see!

In European countries, plug casting tackle is so little used as to be practically nonexistent. The fly rod and the spinning rod are favorites, and have been so for many years. From Stockholm to Capetown, and on to Bombay and Melbourne, spinning is supremely popular in salt water as well as in fresh.

Although people have been spinning in America to a very minor degree since as long ago as the First World War, the sport's impetus here began in 1932 when Bache Hamilton Brown began to import French equipment and later to promote and to manufacture the tackle. Bache was a neighbor of mine for several years. We often went spinning together, and I am most grateful to him for influencing my early interest in this fascinating way to fish.

A great deal of misconception has been born of our calling this sport "spinning" when it is not so called in other countries. This is particularly true because in England there is a very different method of angling which also is called "spinning." The English use the word to identify a means of casting lures that (usually) spin, using reels predominantly of the revolving spool type and longer rods with heavier lines. English spinning is more akin to our own bait casting, and frequently calls for the use of prawns, minnows or other live or preserved baits, oftentimes sewn or impaled on a wire and spinner device (with multiple hooks) which causes the bait to revolve in the water. Plugs and relatively heavy metal lures also are used extensively. In light spinning, many of the rods and reels are almost identical with our own plug casting tackle and, for all general purposes, English spinning and American plug casting or bait casting are very nearly the same.

What we call "spinning" here is termed "thread-line" fishing there, so it will be seen that American spinning and English spinning are quite different. "Thread-line" or "fixed-spool" fishing is very popular in England as well as in most other foreign countries, and is almost exactly the same as the spinning with which we are becoming more and more familiar. When they refer to what looks to us like plug casting gear as "spinning equipment," it is quite natural that many Americans wonder just what it is all about. I agree with many that the appellation "spinning," therefore, is unfortunate, and that we should have adopted the English term "thread-line" or should have called our spinning something else. But the word "spinning" has come into common usage; evidently it is too late to change it.

Another repercussion of this mix-up in nomenclature is the fact that some few American manufacturers, perhaps innocently, have advertised certain reels and rods (reels particularly) as being proper for spinning when in fact they are not so at all, or are only remotely so at best. Many of these reels are uncommonly good ones for plug casting or bait fishing, and many of them are true first cousins of spinning reels because the line casts from a fixed spool instead of from a revolving one. Many of them have a cover or "funneling device" concealing the reel spool, thus demanding that the line be released through a small aperture in the center of the cover. Reels of this sort may add a bit of symmetry to what sometimes is considered to be an awkward design. But when the line spool is thus covered, or when the speed of the uncoiling line is impeded by the reel in any way, the reel is not a spinning reel in the truest sense of the word.

This point, I know, will be disputed, through previous misconception in this country, and so I should like to comment upon it briefly. The principal advantage of the true spinning reel is that casting from the fixed spool allows the line to uncoil with an absolute minimum of friction. This helps to make it possible for the reel to be used in casting weighted lures which are too small and too light to be handled successfully with any other type of reel. We know that when a small butt (or gathering) guide, rather than a larger one, is used on the rod, this reduces casting distance rather drastically. With identical tackle, except for a change in this guide, it has been noted that the smaller guide cuts down casting distance by as much as 30 per cent. Therefore it follows, when an even smaller aperture (even as small as a shoelace eyelet) is a part of the cover of an enclosed spool reel, and is so very close to the uncoiling line, that this restriction to the unimpeded flow of the line must decrease casting distance even more.

By this, I do not mean to discount the advantages of the covered spool type of fixed spool reel. Even if these reels did nothing more for the angler than to eliminate the nuisance of backlashes, their existence would be justified. Many of these reels cast beautifully when heavier lures are used. But when we consider such reels as spinning reels, we are digressing from spinning in its truest sense. As this is written I know of more than one hundred orthodox spinning reels which are made in Europe; and I know of none of them which are equipped with covered spools. The covered spool reel is an American development. I do not intend to minimize its good points when I concur with the international opinion that such reels are not orthodox in spinning. One has to draw the line somewhere and, lest we become confused by wandering too far afield, it seems logical to confine this book to the discussion of spinning tackle of purely conventional types and to rely upon its readers to decide as they wish about the rest.

Spinning in America suffered rather badly from growing pains in its formative years. Americans have developed plug casting tackle to a position of world eminence. Europeans did the same thing for spinning gear. And yet we Americans blithely scanned the foreign research of years in spinning, and immediately attempted to "improve" upon it. The majority of American "improvements" have been far from such. Some of them have been confusing, confounding and annoying to American anglers. Now that the smoke has cleared somewhat, it is interesting to observe that we have made no improvements of any consequence in foreign spinning reels and none in foreign monofilament lines. We have, however, made improvements in braided lines, in lures, and to a very large extent in rods.

In its formative years, most Americans looked upon spinning with considerable skepticism. "It is a flash in the pan and will soon die out" and "It is a deadly method which will deplete our waters of fish" were two remarks often quoted. The fallacy of the first now is obvious. In areas where fishermen understand the proper tackle and tactics for spinning, there is no type of fishing which ever has enjoyed more sensational growth. In America, spinning today shares prominence with fly-fishing and plug casting as being one of the three major angling methods. And its popularity still is increasing. Even a child can learn to use the tackle quickly. But the accomplished spinning angler soon realizes that, while anyone can learn easily to have fun and to catch fish with this gear, the fine points of the sport can make it fully as demanding of skill as dry-fly fishing, and with a far greater latitude of usefulness.

With spinning gear we can cast baits of all types, spinners, spoons, flies, nymphs and plugs. We can cast most of them farther than with any other tackle. We can cast them more easily and fully as accurately, without the nuisance of backlashes. We can use tackle so light that we give the fish as much of a sporting chance as we desire; and we can add immeasurably to the thrills of angling thereby.

The great latitude in the adaptability of spinning tackle has previously caused the comment that the method is "deadly" and that its use would deplete our streams and lakes of fish. Now we know that this is not so. Spinning is very effective on big waters or when streams are high and discolored, such as during the spring season. At other times and in other places the fly rod is more effective. There are conditions when plug casting tackle is superior to either. Let us recognize that spinning has so many advantages that every angler should own the tackle; but let's not go overboard about it. Other types of gear have their places, too, and this always should be so. Much as I love spinning, I should hate to think that I ever would have to give up my fly rods!

Some of the state Fish and Game Commissions have wondered what, if any, restrictions should be put on the use of spinning tackle. Some even have considered outlawing it altogether. Now it generally is recognized that spinning is no more "deadly" than other forms of fishing, and that restrictions, if any, should be as to how the method is used, rather than against the method itself. Most broad-minded spinning anglers agree that certain waters should be restricted to fly-fishing only. In other places they agree that waters should be restricted to the use of artificial lures, or even to the use of lures with single hooks. Such restrictions can be made when need be. The type of rod, reel and line which is used is relatively unimportant.

Part of the stigma which the uninitiated placed on spinning was caused by our importation of treble-hooked lures from abroad, where treble-hooked lures (and even gangs of treble hooks on lures) are very popular. Influenced by this, most American manufacturers equipped their lures with treble hooks also. It is satisfying to note, as we come of age in spinning, that the use of treble hooks is beginning to decline. Anglers are learning that they can hook and hold just as many fish on single hooks as they can on trebles; in fact, many maintain the single hook to be superior for this. They are learning that treble hooks are a nuisance to untangle in the tackle box and in the net, and that they are more difficult to remove from fishes' mouths. There is no question but that the single hook normally is more sensible and more sporting, particularly when fishing for trout and other of our more "aristocratic" species.

Thus even in the field of small plugs, which are so popular in spinning, the series of treble hooks is giving way to single trebles, and single trebles are giving way to the single hook only. All this is most encouraging to sportsmen, and it helps greatly in improving the prestige of spinning. Several states have outlawed all but small single hooks on trout streams, and there are few who will not admit that this progressive step makes spinning more sporting and no less productive. By this means, we can release more harmlessly the fish we do not need and those which are too small, keeping only a few of the larger ones with which to decorate the skillet.

Since *Spinning for American Game Fish* was published in 1947, the growth of the sport has been amazing. It is a source of great satisfaction to me that so many thousands of anglers found that first book of mine helpful. I trust that they will find this new one equally so.

And now, with best wishes for your success — Let's go spinning!

J. D. B., Jr.

Longmeadow, Massachusetts

SPINNING

for Fresh Water *Game Fish*

CHAPTER ONE

Let's Go Spinning

SPINNING TACKLE often provides all the difference between enjoying a good day's fishing and not catching anything at all. Among many examples of this, I particularly remember the week we spent on Oregon's Deschutes River fishing for steelhead.

We pitched camp a mile or so above where the turbulent stream enters the Columbia, near The Dalles. From here on, black cliffs spewed volcanic boulders into the wide river, which swirled darkly in oily blackness when the sun passed over the mountain wall. Reports were that a new run of big fish was on its way upstream from the sea, so we put our tackle together hurriedly for an hour or two of evening fishing.

The fly rod man was one of the most accomplished at his art in the world. With him, distance casting records and prize fish were commonplace. The other two of the four anglers were local boys, and they both knew the ropes.

"Better leave that fly rod in its case and try spinning," one of them advised. "The river is fast and the fish are near the bottom. A fly won't get down to them."

The fly rod man kept on stringing his rod and looked at his three iconoclastic companions with disdain and pity.

"Guess I can manage it," he grunted. "Never used a spinning rod and I guess I never shall. Want to take a little bet on the biggest fish?"

"Even money that with your fly rod you don't take anything at all," one of the local boys said brashly. "If you don't agree, it's like I was taking candy from a baby!"

"You'll never get a dime from this baby," the fly rod man said. "I'll buy all the steak you can eat if I don't trim your pants off! And that goes for the rest of you jewelry tossers, too." He took his rod and stalked to the river in righteous indignation.

We watched his beautiful power casts from the corners of our eyes. Instinctively he knew all the likely holding positions for the fish, and his flies covered spot after spot, regardless of distance.

"Fish on!" one of the spinning anglers called, as he leaned into his rod against the fast run of the steelhead.

"Tallyho!" cried the other.

Both fish jumped at the same time. Both were big ones.

The fly-rod man kept on casting. . . .

The evening score was seven good-sized fish for the three spinning rods, but not even a strike for the fly.

"Tomorrow's another day," the fly rod man said.

"Luck has had its hour; you chaps need taking down a bit."

He was up at early light, industriously fishing while we made coffee on the portable stove. He cast tirelessly all the day through, but when darkness came he had drawn a blank.

"You've got to get your lure deeper," someone commented. "The score is nineteen to zero, and the biggest fish is twelve pounds. Try spinning. Bump the bottom with your lure, and you'll catch fish!"

"You stick to your racket and I'll stick to mine," the fly rod man answered doggedly. "There's a new day coming."

The new day came and went, and at the end of the fifth day the result was the same. The fly rod man's determination was heart-rending. No one could have handled his tackle better. But the rivalry between the exponents of the two types of gear had faded away for lack of contest.

I rigged a spare spinning outfit and left it, invitingly conspicuous, near his place at dinner. All of us ignored his side glances in its direction.

Next morning he had a change of heart. He left his fly rod where it was and picked up the spinning rod.

"Guess maybe I'll borrow this contraption a few minutes and try a few casts," he said. "Come on down and show me how." Then he added, "Gee, but I'd like to catch a steelhead!"

He learned to handle the tackle quickly and disappeared upstream. Half an hour later he tried to conceal a grin as he returned with a beautiful eight- pound fish.

"More fun than I thought," he admitted. "Seems fairly sporty, too."

"What size tippet were you using on your fly rod leader?" I asked him.

"Six pounds."

"How strong do you think the whole line is, on your spinning rod?"

"How strong is it?"

"It's four pounds test," I answered.

"Gee!" he exclaimed. "And I leaned into him a bit, too!"

He used the spinning rod all the rest of the day, and he caught several nice steelhead. He used it later during our trip, and has been doing so often and successfully ever since.

His experience on the Deschutes is fairly typical of the fact that spinning frequently pays off when nothing else will. Undoubtedly, there are many who read this who at the moment may prefer other types of tackle. On occasion, so do I. Nevertheless, it is very valuable for all anglers to learn the facts about spinning.

Fishermen who never have watched a reasonably accomplished spinning angler in action have a pleasant surprise in store for them. He may be standing in front of (or even under) trees and bushes in a spot from which a fly fisherman could not cast to any distance at all. Yet, with a flip of his wrist (and no need for a backcast) he can send his tiny lure far out into the stream or lake, accurately placing it wherever he wishes it to land. He even can poke his rod through a hole in the foliage at the water's edge and from this difficult place he can flip his lure to a satisfying distance. And let's remember that, while such bushy places may not be the most convenient from which to fish, they oftentimes are the most productive, because few fly rod anglers or bait casters can, or will, try to fish from them.

All of us can think of such locations. One of my favorites is on the wide and deep lower reaches of Massachusetts's Deerfield River, where the bank is steep and heavily overgrown with large bushes. Anglers have made a path bypassing the spot completely. Yet the river forms a minor channel here, running amid large rocks, and a small spring trickles in from the high bank. Large trout find food and protection in this pool, and are relatively undisturbed by anglers. From a precarious footing along the ledgy bank the spinning angler can flip his lure under or between the tangle of foliage to reach the outer edge of the little channel. As the lure sinks and swings downstream it is a rare day when a goodly trout will not flash out to take it.

The most successful spinning fishermen I know of

make a habit of finding and remembering such hard-to-fish-from places. A mental map of half a dozen of them usually is the key to a successful day astream. So — when passage along the bank becomes so difficult that most fishermen bypass the place, it often is profitable to investigate it thoroughly. Maybe it is a "hot spot" in disguise!

If the spinning angler enjoys using worms or other bait, he can flip it far out into the stream without having to add lead to his line, unless he wishes to do so. Tiny baits can be cast much farther with spinning tackle than with a fly or bait casting rod, and with only a fraction of the effort. The spinning fisherman, with the aid of a little plastic ball (which we shall describe later on) can use wet flies or nymphs very successfully, and there are ways of using dry flies which would breed envy in the dry-fly fishermen themselves! If he wishes to drift his bait or fly down through a pool or over a weed bed, the plastic ball will help him to fish it at any depth he desires — and will aid him in casting the tiny lures to distances which nearly are unbelievable!

When the fish are feeding near the surface, the spinning angler can fish for them there. When they are deep down in pools or runs, or back of rocks in fast water, the spinning lure can reach down to them. The spinning lure can attract them even when the stream is high and discolored, enabling the spinning angler to catch fish when the fly rod man is unsuccessful.

After even less than an hour of practice, the spinning angler can learn enough to go out and catch fish,
even though the finer points of his sport may be somewhat more involved. He can teach spinning quickly to
his wife and children, thus aiding their fun as well as
protecting his own. I've seen husbands become extremely annoyed with the attempts of their wives to
use a fly rod, and I am of the opinion that their conversion to spinning tackle has helped to avoid many
disturbances in the families of fishermen!

Do these pleasant prospects explain why the spinning angler usually catches more fish than does his
brothers with the fly rod or the plug casting outfit?
Yes — but there's more to it than that!

Experience shows that more big fish, and more of
the smaller ones, too, are caught with relatively tiny
lures than are caught with larger ones. The fixed spool
reel makes these tiny lures especially practical. Furthermore, the spinning reel allows the use of extremely
fine lines, with a minimum of danger of breakage.
These fine lines, inconspicuous as the tippet on a fly
rod leader, are less noticeable to fish and therefore
the fish are the more easily attracted to the lure. The
fine lines are easier to cast and they make less commotion on the surface, at the same time being less noticeable underneath.

The observation often is made that a fisherman cannot catch fish unless his line is in the water! The spinning angler never needs to make false casts, as does the fly rod man. He can cast quickly and easily, thus covering more territory. The fine line and the lack of necessity of picking it up from the water after inadequate casts mean that the spinning man is actually fishing more of the time, and with less chance of scaring the fish. Naturally, this should improve his chances of success. A somewhat similar comparison can be made between the spinning angler and the plug caster, with the latter's tendency to backlashes, his larger, heavier lures and his larger, heavier line.

We cannot, however, thus describe the benefits of spinning without dealing more fairly with the other two methods. I was a fly-fisherman long before I began to enjoy spinning, and I still am a fly-fisherman today. When a hatch is on the stream, my spinning outfit is left at home, because when fish are nymphing or surface feeding on insects, the fly rod remains supreme. I always have enjoyed plug casting, too, and realize that when bass are near the weed beds the plug rod may be superior to the spinning rod. But in this latter comparison I must admit that spinning tackle has weaned me away from my plug rods rather successfully. It has done the same for other anglers, too! Spinning bridges a much needed gap in angling, but the most fortunate fisherman is the one who understands all three methods. Each one has qualities peculiar to itself and it is everyone's pleasant option to decide which type of tackle he wishes to use to accomplish whatever type of fishing comes to hand.

It is good that the rudiments of spinning are easy to learn, because fishing is a form of recreation, and the enjoyment of one's recreation should not have to become an ordeal of practice. But after this introduction comes the study of the finer points of the sport, which perhaps is why it is so appealing to the expert angler as well as to the novice. When the essentials have been learned, we can devote added seasons to perfecting accurate casting; to learning how to catch truly big fish with the most delicate of tackle; to studying how to balance our tackle properly for longest, easiest casts; to finding out how to select the proper lures for the water to be fished and for the fish to be caught, and how to operate them in the most enticing manner.

To illustrate how far we can go: In France, and in some other countries, the true spinning expert rarely will deign to use lines of conventional strength and lures of conventional weight. There, they enjoy a sort of postgraduate division of the sport called *ultra-léger*, or extremely light casting. Wandlike rods and the smallest reels are used, with lines often testing less than a pound and with lures so small that they weigh less than a sixteenth of an ounce. With this tiny tackle they seek very large fish, and if the weight of the fish is not better than ten times the breaking strength of the line they do not regard their catch very highly.

This means that it is considered quite sportsman-like to land a ten-pound fish with a one-pound-test line, or a fifty-pound fish with a five-pound-test line — a feat which most of us will agree is sporting in the extreme!

How do they do it? Briefly, they use the smallest, sharpest hooks in order to strike the fish effectively, and then they attempt to keep the fish moving under the constant irritation of the barb. By expertly guid-ing him whenever possible, they allow the fish to sub-due himself by his own activity, with an absolute minimum of force exerted by the angler! Feats such as this are quite obviously impossible with all species of fish, and feasible only in favorable places. However, they have been accomplished in more cases than might be imagined, and the method (which will be described in more detail later) offers a rather impos-ing challenge to all true anglers.

Thus, when the remark sometimes is made that "spinning is not very sporty" it is rather clear that whoever makes it is relatively unacquainted with the subject. Undoubtedly this is because the majority of spinning fishermen use lines much stronger than they need to, and lures much too heavy and too large. In so doing they sacrifice a great deal of the pleasure and of the rewards of spinning, as we later shall see.

Another rather erroneous remark often heard is that "spinning is just another form of bait or plug casting." It is true that some of the lures which can be used with one method also can be used with the other, but there the similarity seems to end. The tackle and tactics of spinning are as different from plug casting and from fly-fishing as the two latter methods are different from each other.

Spinning, basically, is the art of fishing with the fixed spool reel; while plug casting normally employs the revolving spool reel. In order to understand the sport more fully, it may be well to take a minute to describe the principles of the reel involved. This is most easily explained by the perhaps too familiar simile of the spool of thread.

When we slip the spool over a pencil and pull on the thread, we cause the spool to revolve. This is the principle of the plug casting reel, but in the plug casting reel we have some rather necessary gears and other moving parts which must be started in motion each time a cast is made. The spool must overcome friction against the shaft, and it also must overcome its own inertia. Even when the reel is precisely made, as so many are, the rapid rotation caused by long casts makes the resultant drag significant. To minimize this drag, we need heavier lures to pull out the line and we need a stronger line to protect the tackle from breakage. Backlashes are caused with this type of reel, because the angler does not stop the rotation of

the spool quickly enough as the lure lands. This causes
the spool to overrun and wind the line back on itself,
frequently making a bad snarl.

Now, let's examine the spinning principle. If we
hold the spool of thread in our fingers by one end, we
can pull the thread off the other end almost without
any friction at all. This uncoiling of the line is the
basic principle of spinning. To reduce friction even
more, the spool of most spinning reels oscillates in and
out, to cross-wind the line. This automatic crisscrossing of the line prevents coils from catching between
one another. When this is so, a smooth line nearly will
drop off the spool, even with no weight to aid it. Now,
all we have to do is to provide a method of winding
the line back onto the spool, and a method of braking
the spool to provide adjustable resistance to the paying out of the line when a fish is hooked. When we
have done this, we have a spinning reel. Since the line
uncoils from a fixed spool, instead of unrolling from a
revolving one, the line on the spinning reel cannot
overrun. Therefore, backlashes are eliminated entirely.

The principle of the spinning reel goes back into the
seventeenth century, when Swiss anglers — and even
some northwestern American Indians, independently
— learned how to cast a line (connected to a weight)
from a wooden frame on which it was wound. Later,
the Scotch accomplished the same thing by coiling the

casting line in a flat basket attached around their
waists, casting it out with the aid of a rod. The "belly
winder," or belt reel, is a present-day development of
this and evidently first was used by the Swiss.

In the eighteenth century the French learned to
cast their line from a large drum made of wooden
spindles which looked very much like a line dryer.
This contrivance was affixed at one end to a stick,
which was held in one hand while the abnormally
long wooden rod was held in the other. The line cast
from this device passably well, but it had to be recovered by hand. Vicomte Henri de France improved on
this considerably, by making the drum smaller and
by attaching it to the rod in much the same manner as
a spinning reel is attached today. After the cast, the
best way he could contrive to get the line back on the
reel was to wind it on by hand, using a device made
like a large crocheting needle. This was done along
about 1900 and so is a relatively modern invention.
From all this it will be obvious that our predecessors
had their full share of trials and tribulations!

Vicomte Henri's development thus had some of the
attributes of a modern spinning reel. Just before this,
in 1884, a Scottish fisherman named Peter Malloch
developed a "Turn Table" type of metal reel, wherein
the line was cast off a fixed spool which greatly resem-
bled the size and shape of the old-fashioned tele-
phone mouthpiece. To recover line, the reel spool was
swiveled to a right angle to the rod, thus enabling the

line to be wound on by means of a handle on the rotating reel spool. Such reels commonly were made by hand in France shortly after this. They were of the crudest sort, without multiplying action, since they were made by individual hand craftsmanship. The reel had so many faults that fishermen were greatly relieved when improvements were made. Most particularly, the reel in casting put a twist in the line every time a coil left the spool, as it does in our spinning reels today. But our reel winds on the line in the same manner that it came off, thus automatically removing the twist. The Malloch and Turn Table reels did not do this, because they had to recover line on a rotating spool. Consequently, each cast put more and more twist in the line, very soon subjecting the fisherman to a rather discouraging mess. They knew a few tedious ways of removing the twist, but that is beside the point. I have gone into slight detail about this type of reel because there are modern adaptations of it being sold in this country today. The principle was discarded in Europe as being impractical several generations ago.

The dawn of the golden age of spinning came with the development of the Illingworth reel, and also with the invention of nylon lines. Mr. Alfred Holden Illingworth was an English cotton-mill owner who undoubtedly was influenced by the developments of Peter Malloch and of Henri de France. Probably he was influenced even more by watching thread spin or spi-

ral from the cotton-spinning frames in his mills. In any
event, in 1905 he patented and later commercially
manufactured a true spinning reel with a manual
pickup on a revolving cup, but without a cross-
winding device. Later, he improved upon this reel,
and so did others. Today, in Europe alone, no less
than seventy manufacturers produce modern spinning reels, and their use by anglers is numbered in the
millions!

Spinning lines passed through an equally gradual
and painful development. The early ones were
braided of cotton, silk or linen. These became waterlogged unless dressed continually, and, even if they
were dried carefully after each use, they deteriorated
in strength due to rotting and abrasion to the extent
that they were extremely undependable.

Japanese (or artificial) gut lines were a later development, made from silk thread coated with the se-
cretion of the silkworm. When dry, "Jap gut" was wiry
and unyielding and so it was necessary to soak it
before each use. After soaking, it was almost too pliable and it deteriorated so fast in strength that a season's service was about all that one could expect. The
line had many other faults, but it was inexpensive
and had the additional advantage of being relatively
invisible in the water. Even before the Second World
War, the advent of the greatly superior nylon had rel-
egated it into disuse.

A similar transition can be noted in the evolution

of the spinning rod. In the early days of European spinning, rods of twelve feet or more in length and weighing in the vicinity of fifteen ounces were common. These were made of several types of hard woods, such as greenheart from British Guiana, ironwood from Brazil, lancewood from Great Britain and the heartwood of South American palm and American hickory. They were actually heavy-duty fly rods which, with the improvement of spinning reels, grew shorter in length and lighter in weight as the years progressed, finally culminating in the delicate, efficient but powerful weapons with which we are familiar today.

Today, we can visit almost any tackle store and select our choice of lures from hundreds on display. Compare this with the early days of spinning, when most of the lures were of the live bait type which required painstaking care to rig properly for anything approaching efficient use. First, you had to go out and catch your bait, whether shrimps, crayfish or minnows. Then, lest it spoil on the way to the stream, you had to pickle it in a solution of formalin. You cut and bent tiny spinners or propellers of metal, rigged them with wire traces and hooks, and sewed, tied or impaled the bait to the resulting apparatus. Nor was a great gob of worms often forgotten. The purists of the era dressed weighted salmon flies, and spinning lures made entirely of metal (such as the Devon) gradually evolved.

Compare all this with the beautifully matched and truly efficient equipment which we have today! When we do so we may wonder how these anglers of earlier years could have had the patience to build their own tackle (as so many had to do) and to use it with pleasure and success under the difficulties they experienced. Undoubtedly the comparison is purely relative. There has been so much progress in the last few years that I hate to reflect upon what other anglers will have to say about our tackle in the years to come. In any event, our spinning gear is extremely suitable to its purposes and we can be content with it the way it is, even though we constantly are experimenting to improve it, as did so many other fishermen in the past.

One question asked most frequently is "How far can one cast with spinning tackle?"

In 1908, Mr. Illingworth used his specially built tournament tackle and reel (the Illingworth No. 1) to throw a three-dram (three-eighths-ounce) weight to a distance of three hundred and nine feet, at the International Casting Tournament of that year. In 1951, a California spinning fisherman using orthodox fishing tackle cast a three-eighths-ounce lure to a distance of two hundred and thirteen feet and a one-ounce lure to three hundred and thirty feet for modern records at the La Palma Casting Club, of Anaheim, California. It is encouraging to know that such casts can be made, and, with the constant improvements going on in tackle, it is almost certain that these latter records soon will be improved rather decisively. Few anglers have any need or desire to cast to such distances, since it is a well-known axiom that one should only cast far enough to reach the fish and that the farther one has to cast, the less chance one has of hooking whatever prize may take a fancy to his lure.

Another question asked almost as often as these others is "Can fly-fishing or plug casting tackle be adapted to use with spinning gear?"

If one element of the tackle is more important than any other, it is the spinning reel. It is highly worth while to invest in a good one, having the qualities which will be discussed in the next chapter. Fortunately, good ones are not necessarily expensive. Without an efficient spinning reel, it is impossible fully to enjoy spinning. Small diameter, lightweight nylon braided or monofilament lines will function on such a reel, regardless of whether these lines are sold as spinning lines, plug casting lines or something else. However, it is much safer to buy well recommended lines made especially for spinning, for reasons which will become apparent as we go along. In the matter of rods, there is a bit of leeway. One can fit an adapter handle to his plug casting tip and have a makeshift spinning rod. One can fasten the same handle to the tip section of a two-piece fly rod or to the tip and middle sections of a three-piece rod, and can enjoy spinning to a degree with this contrivance. This may do as a temporary expedient, but the distribution of power, the length, and the sizes and placing of the guides on fly rods and plug rods make their conversion to spinning rods impractical. The equipment can be used after a fashion, but it is at best a very poor substitute for tackle made correctly for the purpose. Adapter handles cost in the vicinity of five dollars, and it always has seemed to me more desirable to save this money toward the purchase of a truly efficient spinning rod.

Lures are another matter entirely. Many of the smaller ones made for plug casting are ideal for spinning. If their weight and casting qualities are suitable, they should serve the purpose quite nicely — and it even is possible for us to make certain types at home if we have a few tools, a bit of knowledge and sufficient inclination.

One of the greatest drawbacks to the enjoyment of spinning during recent years has been the innocent acceptance by anglers of whatever spinning tackle dealers decided to sell to them. Usually, the fisherman goes to his dealer and asks merely for a spinning outfit, without disclosing where or for what he wishes to use it. No experienced fly-fisherman would ask for a fly-fishing outfit that way! Innocent purchases on the dealer's part frequently have provided him with ill-chosen equipment which he must sell. This perhaps should not be blamed to the tackle store, but the result is that it is the innocent fisherman who suffers. All too often he is sold an inefficient reel when he could have bought a very good one for the same price, or less. He is sold a rod which may be improper in action and strength, a line which does not fit the rod, and a collection of lures toward which no self-respecting fish would direct a second glance.

This state of affairs fortunately is not so in all cases. Many dealers have made a business of studying spinning and have equipped themselves with an ample assortment of very good tackle. Their advice is sound and is to be respected. Fortunate is the fisherman who puts his trust in one of these; and luckily their number is increasing. After having attempted to straighten out numerous fiascos in the selection of spinning tackle, it is my fervent hope that this book will enable its readers to make intelligent purchases and then that it will aid them in obtaining from their new equipment the maximum of pleasure and of profitable use.

No single spinning outfit is ideal for all purposes, any more than is a single fly-casting outfit. A rod of proper power should be selected for the type of fishing for which it will be used most, and to it should be fitted a line (or lines) in the correct strength range to suit both the rod and the weight-range of lures to be used. Doubtless the reel will hold sufficient line, but it must have many other qualities as well. Buying a good spinning outfit is one thing, and buying a properly balanced or properly mated outfit is quite another. Both are most necessary if we are to enjoy to the fullest the many benefits of spinning.

CHAPTER TWO

About Spinning Reels

WHEN ONE FIRST LOOKS at a spinning reel, the impression often is that it appears to be a rather awkward contrivance. As we become accustomed to it, however, it seems obvious that each element of its design has a definite purpose which, once understood, transforms its seeming awkwardness into a marvel of efficiency among fishing reels.

It is made to hang under the rod grip because, like a fly reel, it comfortably balances the tackle that way. The reel has a rather long "leg" which keeps the spool far enough away from the rod to allow the line to uncoil without slapping against it. The proper length of the leg also allows the fisherman to control the line comfortably with his forefinger, which is a vital aid to accuracy in spinning. The reel spool faces toward the rod tip to allow the line to uncoil from the spool with a minimum of friction and to pass smoothly through the guides.

We have observed that more than one hundred different varieties of spinning reels now are being manufactured in Europe. The majority of them are being imported into this country and are being distributed so widely that they can be purchased in most regions without difficulty. In addition, a growing number of true spinning reels are being made in the United States. From here and abroad we now may select from a relatively few small ones for light pond and stream fishing; from a large assortment of medium-sized models for average inland angling, and from a moderate number of large and sturdy reels which are a match for the largest surface-fighting fish to be found in the ocean.

Perhaps we can compare spinning reels to people — in that none of them are perfect, while all of them have both good and bad qualities to a greater or lesser degree. Whether we can own only one reel or several, it is important to make a wise choice, because on its wisdom will depend the degree of pleasure and of success which we will enjoy in spinning. Therefore, it seems highly important for every spinning angler, whether beginner or expert, to study the qualities of these various reels so that he will not regret his purchase once it has been made.

The average spinning tackle dealer should be able to show his customer at least half a dozen different models of orthodox spinning reels. He may have sincere rather than ulterior motives for recommending one of them over the others, but in any case it is good insurance for the buyer to be competent to decide for himself.

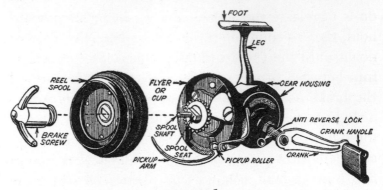

FIGURE 1.

NAMES OF PRINCIPAL PARTS
OF A SPINNING REEL

The names of the parts of a typical spinning reel are shown in Figure 1. Since all reels vary in construction, this drawing identifies the locations of the parts rather than their actual appearance.

BRAKE

The brake screw is a large winged or cupped nut which usually is located in front of the reel spool. It holds the spool on its spindle and it controls the resistance offered by the rotating spool when a fish takes out line. In inspecting the merits of a spinning reel, it is of primary importance to be sure that this brake, or drag, offers sufficient latitude of adjustment; that the drag is smooth, rather than jumpy, and that the brake screw does not slip and thus alter the tension on the line. To check latitude of adjustment, all one has to do is to release the screw until it just begins to take hold; then to count its revolutions while it is screwed down until the spool becomes locked. One complete turn between these extremes is insufficient because, if the brake needs to be adjusted while playing a fish, a slight turn is liable to make the tension too light or too tight, perhaps with disastrous consequences. Two complete turns is satisfactory; some reels offer four or five turns, which seems to be ideal. The degree of brake adjustment may not be overly important when playing small fish, but when a really big one comes along it may mean all the difference between success and failure.

To determine the smoothness of the brake and its nonslipping quality, we must put the line on the reel and preferably rig it to the rod. While one person holds the tackle, the prospective purchaser can pull out a fairly large amount of line, simulating the run of a fish. Try doing this slowly the first time and as fast as possible the second. If the line pulls out smoothly and if the position of the brake screw does not vary in the slightest, it should be safe to approve the reel in so far as the brake is concerned.

I am sure that such a test will not always be convenient in a store, but reputable dealers should allow the angler to try it at home and to return the reel if it is found to be unsatisfactory. In the earlier days of American spinning, we had much more trouble with reel brakes than we do now. I can remember hooking large bonefish, steelhead and bass and having the brake screw give way to the free spool position during the short run of a fish. I can remember other reels whose brakes were so jumpy that the spool would alternately skip and bind during the run. Under such conditions, it is sheer luck if we do not lose the fish. Fortunately, the brakes of the well-known reels are much better today, but some of course are better than others.

Manufacturers have several methods of preventing a brake screw from turning and thus going out of adjustment while a fish is taking out line. Most of these are based on keeping the brake screw from having any contact whatsoever with the reel spool. This often is done by putting a flat side or a groove on the spindle and a corresponding flat side or tooth in the hole of the washer set between brake screw and spool. The revolving spool then cannot make the washer turn and thus influence the brake screw. Sometimes there is another washer between the reel spool and the spool seat on the spindle. This may be of felt, asbestos or metal and usually serves as a cushion to provide greater smoothness and more latitude in the braking qualities of the reel. If a reel brake does not operate properly, it may be because one of the washers has become lost in changing reel spools, or because it has been put on the spindle improperly. These washers are a necessary evil and in many of the newer reels they are an integral part of the brake screw or spool. If a reel is furnished with loose washers, it is wise to remember their proper position and to carry a few spares in case one drops into the water while changing spools for the purpose of putting on the reel a spool containing a more suitable size of line.

QUALITY OF CONSTRUCTION

Of similar importance to a good brake is the smoothness of operation of the reel. One with properly fitted parts will run quietly and easily with the slightest pressure on the handle. If a reel is stiff in its operation, the reason sometimes given is that this is due to the stiffness of the grease in the gear housing. All gear housings are packed with grease, which should make the reel run more easily, rather than the reverse. Gears on inexpensive reels may be die-cast from inferior metals. Their imperfections cause the reel to turn too hard or to be so loose that it is noisy. Poorly made gears also wear out quickly. The gearing mechanism of high grade reels usually is smoothly machine-cut from hard metals and these gears normally are so carefully fitted that the reel operates easily and quietly. Smoothness of operation is a good recommendation for the quality of the parts within, and the reputation of the manufacturer or importer also is important in this respect. The appearance of the exterior is not necessarily an indication of the quality of workmanship inside the reel.

Reels in which the handle can be changed from one

side to the other, for reeling with the opposite hand, usually cannot be made so that the driving gear is doubly pinioned to both sides of the gear housing. If this driving gear is pinioned only to one side, it is apt to cause wobble and consequent noise in the mechanism, particularly after the reel has been used enough for the parts to become worn slightly. Since the sturdiest and most quietly operating reels ordinarily are those of the doubly pinioned type, it is well to inquire about this and to select a reel made either for left-hand or for right-hand reeling, but not for both.

GEAR RATIO

Many buyers of spinning reels inquire about their gear ratio, which usually is between three and four to one. This means that, for every turn of the handle, the cup and pickup make between three and four complete turns. This is not a full indication of the speed of recovery of the line because, in this, the size of the reel spool also must be considered. I have heard inexperienced spinning fishermen (and dealers, too) speak with disfavor about reels with large diameter spools. The large spool, to me, is a distinct and valuable asset because, coupled with a reasonably high gear ratio, it aids materially in quick recovery of line. Quick line-recovery is very important when a fish makes a fast run toward the angler. It is important in fishing shallow streams, in fishing upstream, and sometimes in most effectively working lures or baits. Thus, while a spinning reel may look less streamlined with a larger than normal spool, the larger spool usually has advantages over the smaller one.

A more intelligent yardstick of a reel's efficiency in line recovery is to find out how many inches of line the reel recovers with each turn of the handle. Many of the average-sized reels recover about twenty-five inches of line per turn, which is entirely ample for all normal purposes.

PICKUPS; HOW TO AVOID SNUBBING LINES

The pickup is the part of the reel which engages and guides the line when the line is placed under the control of the reel after making a cast. There are three important types of pickups. One may be standard on one reel, and another on another. A few brands offer an optional choice. These are the *automatic pickup arm,* the *bail pickup* and the *manual* (or finger) *pickup,* as shown in the illustrations of "Typical Spinning Reels."

The *automatic pickup arm* is swung open before the cast is made so that it will not interfere with the uncoiling of the line. When the reel handle is given a partial turn, the pickup arm is tripped by a cam and automatically closes, hooking the line, which slips along it until the line comes in contact with the roller. The arm is of metal which is adequately strong but which can be bent manually. Bending, however, should not be attempted unless the arm operates improperly because of accident or abuse. If it scrapes against the reel spool, it can be bent slightly upward and outward to free it.

On some reels the pickup arm can be operated by a small lever which usually is located at the base of the assembly. While this little gadget undoubtedly has its good points, it does not seem to be particularly necessary, and the majority of reels are not equipped with it. To me, it is just one more part to catch on things and it is more difficult to locate by touch than is the base of the pickup arm. The pickup arm should be opened when it is at the bottom position (farthest away from the rod). This is done by grasping the arm at its base with the thumb and forefinger, pulling it downward to the open position. It is preferable to grasp it at the base rather than nearer its tip in order not to bend it. Opening it can be done very easily, even in the dark.

Before we pass on to something else, it may be helpful to discuss the difficulty which a few fishermen occasionally have of snubbing the line around the pickup arm when making a cast. Some few reels have a tendency to do this, while with others it cannot be done at all. A reason for it is that the tip of the pickup arm extends too far beyond and outward of the front face of the reel spool. Another reason is that the angler may make an erratic and an overly energetic cast, thus causing the line to spiral out improperly and to form too tight a loop, which then may snub itself around the tip of the pickup arm, if it is too long or

The Ru Sport spinning reel
(with the automatic pickup arm)

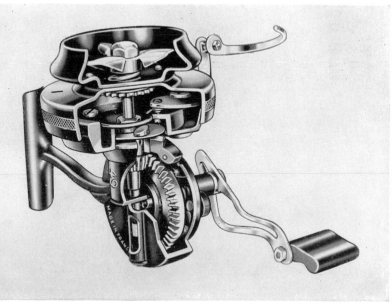

Cutaway view of the Ru Sport
(showing some of the interior parts)

TYPICAL SPINNING REELS

The Mitchell spinning reel
(with the bail pickup)

The Orvis spinning reel
(with the bail pickup)

TYPICAL SPINNING REELS

The Alcedo Micron spinning reel
(small in size, for light casting)

The Martin spinning reel
(an American reel with the bail pickup)

TYPICAL SPINNING REELS

The Airex Mastereel
(an American reel with the automatic pickup arm)

The Record spinning reel
(with the manual pickup)

TYPICAL SPINNING REELS

if it has become bent. Retrieving the line under un-
even tension may contribute to the trouble. One very
popular series of reels has its spools designed with a
specially curved front face. This design eliminates the

FIGURE 2.

SKETCH SHOWING (*left*) HOW LINE CAN SNUB
ITSELF AROUND PICKUP AND (*right*) A SPOOL
DESIGN WHICH PREVENTS IT

difficulty entirely, as shown in Figure 2, and in addition it affords a comfortable and efficient curve
against which the forefinger is placed when stopping
the outward flow of the line.

The *bail pickup* is a spring-activated semicircular
wire rod which is mounted on the revolving cup of the
reel. It is pivoted outward to free the line before a cast
is made. The bail locks in this position, and when the
reel handle is turned a cam and spring automatically
flip it over the front of the spool to engage the line.
This action is similar to that of the automatic pickup
arm in that the line slides along the bail until it comes
in contact with the roller. The bail-type pickup is somewhat more complicated than the arm-type pickup and
therefore is somewhat more prone to get out of order.

If this ever happens it usually is due to the spring (which activates it) pulling from its socket. This makes the bail flap uselessly, putting the reel out of commission. This has happened to me only once in a great many years and, in that case, it was possible to take the mechanism apart and to fix it when we returned to camp that evening. The bail type of pickup does, however, eliminate the possibility of snubbing the line, as above described, and this form of pickup is growing increasingly popular.

The *manual pickup* is the simplest of all three types and consists essentially of a roller affixed to the revolving cup of the reel. The angler's forefinger takes the place of the pickup arm or of the bail. When he wishes to stop the flow of the line (which he should do before the lure drops on the water, in order to keep the line properly tight) he moves his extended forefinger toward his body to a position to the left of the leg of the reel and just under its foot. In this position, he has pulled the line toward him with his forefinger, stopping it from uncoiling. A partial turn of the handle then will cause the roller to catch the line from the forefinger, thereby putting it under control of the reel. This sounds rather complicated, but actually it is extremely easy. Reels with manual pickups are especially popular for salt water fishing, because this element of their mechanism is so simple and foolproof that neither sand nor corrosion can do much harm. This type of pickup often is preferred by advanced casters, but one of the two automatic methods undoubtedly will be easier for the beginner.

NOTES ON THE ROLLER

Each type of pickup has a roller over which the line is retrieved. On some reels the roller is supposed to roll, while on others it is fixed in place for the line to slide over it. The type which is supposed to roll actually does not do so to any great extent. When it becomes worn, it must be replaced. The type which is not supposed to roll has square ends and is fastened in place by means of a screw. When wear occurs, it is a simple matter to remove the screw and to turn the so-called roller to bring a new bearing surface into play. This gives us four bearing surfaces, which leads me to prefer the fixed type over the other. Rollers need to be replaced very rarely, although some types of spinning lines are more abrasive than others. Since a scored roller has a weakening effect upon the line, it is well to install a new one when signs of wear become noticeable.

THE ANTI-REVERSE LOCK

Most reels are equipped with an anti-reverse lock, which prevents the reel handle from backwinding while a fish takes out line. This lock should be disengaged always when making a cast, and usually while operating the lure; but it should be slipped on immediately when a fish becomes hooked. Some anti-reverse locks are more handily placed than others. This device is so necessary that I would not buy any reel unless it has one which operates efficiently and is conveniently placed for instant use. The anti-reverse is controlled by a button or lever, which should be located near the reel handle so that the lever can be thrown on or off instantly without removing the hand from the reel. If this is done, in this manner, there is no chance of the reel's backwinding, which might throw out loose coils to snub themselves around the mechanism. With the anti-backwind device in operation, we can reel in the line; but when the fish decides to make a run we can remove the hand from the reel handle if we want to adjust the brake or to make use of the reel hand to provide auxiliary braking power. This device also is a vital aid in trolling, or in still-fishing with spinning tackle. The rod can be held with one hand, or in a rod support, making it unnecessary to give the tackle much attention until after a fish has taken the lure.

REEL SPOOLS

In addition to the previously mentioned advantage of the relatively large-diameter spool in affording quicker recovery of line, I think that the larger spool offers a certain amount of advantage in making longer casts. When we cast off line, the longer the cast the more the line draws upon its reserve in the spool. The deeper the line sinks below the lip of the spool, the greater is the casting force needed to pull it up over the lip. Quite obviously, a larger spool, with its greater circumference, draws upon the depth of this reserve less than does a smaller spool. This means less drag and therefore longer casts.

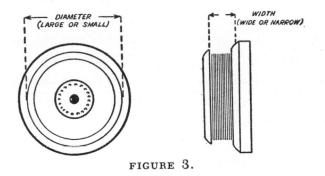

FIGURE 3.

WIDTH AND DIAMETER OF A REEL SPOOL

Of course, the width of the spool (see Figure 3) has a similar relationship to the spool's reserve of line. Most average-sized reels have spools whose inside (line) width is between three-eighths and half an inch. If the spool of the reel we are considering is wider than this, the same result will be achieved as with the larger diameter, but narrower, spool. Very wide spools, however, have the disadvantage that the cross-winding of the line must be mechanically perfect to prevent the line casting off occasionally in a snarl of coils. This is why more reels are made with relatively narrow spools than with relatively wide ones.

Spinning reel spools usually are made of metal or

of reinforced plastic. It is important that they should be strongly built; some of the plastic spools are not. Nylon lines are relatively elastic and, when wound in under excess tension, will cause the accumulating tight coils to constrict and build up a force sufficient to burst a weakly constructed spool. This happened twice while I was fishing for steelhead with a certain type of reel, before I learned to pump in the fish properly to avoid winding the line too tightly on the spool. After I had regained a large amount of line, all of a sudden the sides of the spool parted company and coils of line flew in all directions. Needless to say, I lost the steelhead, and both line and spool were ruined. By proper reeling I could have avoided all this. The same thing has happened to others when using insufficiently strong reel spools. So it is well to examine the strength of the spool, regardless of the material of which it is made.

Unless one is fishing for sport fish which may make extremely long runs, the line capacity of nearly all reels is more than adequate. Most reels of average size will hold at least two hundred yards of three-pound-test line, or at least one hundred and fifty yards of six-pound-test line. In the rare cases when more line is thought to be needed, it may be well to restrict the purchase to reels having extra large capacity, but it does not seem necessary otherwise.

When you are buying a reel, I should like to recommend that you purchase one or two extra reel spools. It always is well to have a choice of at least two sizes or strengths of line, and it is good insurance to carry a spare.

ADVANTAGES OF CROSS-WINDING THE LINE

When we turn the handle of the reel, an eccentric element in the driving gear causes the reel's spindle to move backwards and forwards, thus causing the reel spool attached to the spindle to do the same thing. This cross-winds the line on the reel to prevent coils of line from catching between others in casting.

FIGURE 4.

SKETCH ILLUSTRATING CROSS-WINDING
OF LINE ON A REEL SPOOL

Note that one complete revolution of the reel handle causes the spool of the reel to oscillate backward and forward through one full cycle. If the reel has a four-to-one gear ratio (which is a bit more than average), the reel will wind on two coils of line while going forward and two more while going backward, with each complete turn of the reel handle. Assuming that the spool has an effective width of half an inch (which also is a bit more than average), it will be seen that the coils are wound on the reel with each two criss-crossing a quarter of an inch apart. Actually, however, the gear ratio is not an even number, such as 4 to 1, but rather is a fractional number, such as 3.58 to 1. The result of this little detail is that the line progressively crisscrosses around the entire circumference of the spool rather than all in one place. Ideal cross-winding applies the coils far enough apart so that they will not catch between each other in casting, yet so that they will be compactly placed for greatest line capacity on the spool. All this may be of somewhat minor interest, but I wish to make the important point that the line must cross-wind adequately enough to accomplish the above result.

Once in a while we find a reel in which reeling will cause the line to pile up on the back or on the front of the spool, rather than winding on evenly. This is caused by the spool's being fastened a trifle too far forward, or too far back, on the spindle. On some reels, the ratchet assembly which positions the spool on the spindle can be loosened and adjusted to put the spool in the proper location on the spindle for even reeling of line. In other cases, this is a minor job for a skilled spinning-reel repairman. Anglers rarely encounter this difficulty because reels nearly always are properly adjusted. In rarer cases the trouble may be due to the pickup arm support's having become bent, or to improper placement of washers on the spindle.

There are a few types of small-capacity reels which do not have (and do not need to have) a cross-winding device. These are the reels with ultra-large diameter and extremely narrow spools. In these reels the spools are so narrow that cross-winding is relatively ineffective and therefore it is eliminated. Reels with spools of this sort are best for ultra-light line fishing. While some of them operate beautifully, they have not yet become very popular.

THE LEG AND THE FOOT

These parts of the reel usually are an integral casting with the gear housing. The foot enables the reel to be secured to the rod, while the leg keeps the reel spool at a sufficient distance from the rod so that the line will not slap against it in casting. Spinning reels are made with various designs of legs. Some of these are more conducive to comfort and to efficiency in casting than are others. Before buying a reel, it is advisable to fasten it to a rod and to operate it (with or without line) to determine how comfortably it fits the angler's hand. This can be done quite conveniently at the same time that one tests the brake, the whole operation taking but a very few minutes.

HOW TO GRASP THE TACKLE

Grasp the outfit with two fingers in front of the leg and with two fingers behind it and see if the extended forefinger can touch the front face of the reel spool comfortably as illustrated later in "Casting Positions." This is most important in efficient and accurate casting. If this way of holding the reel does not seem comfortable, try putting only one finger ahead of the leg, and then try three. One of these three ways of grasping the reel should result in a hold where the tip of the forefinger can touch the front face of the spool comfortably and securely. This correct hold will vary depending on the design of the reel and the size of the angler's hand. The number of fingers ahead of, and behind, the leg is unimportant, although most fishermen think that two ahead and two behind are preferable. The important thing is to obtain a comfortable grasp with correct forefinger position.

Now, turn the reel handle a bit while operating the pickup. If the hand stays free from contact with moving parts, and if we have found an efficient way to grasp the reel, we can pass on it from this point of view. One design of reel may be handier for an individual than are others, just as is a favorite shotgun to a gunner.

In perusing these various rather detailed (and probably somewhat boring) points, one should not draw the impression that spinning reels are difficult to select or that they habitually get out of order. I have tried to be somewhat explicit in describing them in the hope that this will aid in the selection of a proper one. A well-made spinning reel rarely gets out of order and, if it does, this usually is due to errors of the angler rather than of the manufacturer. Several of these errors happen rather frequently and, since they are so easily avoidable, it has seemed well worth while to discuss them in whatever detail is necessary.

As a summary of all this: Select a reel from those of proper size and price range, first being sure that the brake operates properly. Then, if the reel seems to run smoothly and if there is a good anti-reverse lock on it, the other points mentioned may be treated with whatever consideration the fisherman desires.

LEFT-HANDED REELS

Spinning tackle usually is made for casting with the right hand and for reeling with the left. It is incorrect and very inefficient to change hands, as we do while plug casting, or in some cases while fly-fishing.

Frequently, left-handed casters say: "I never could operate the tackle that way. Can't I buy a left-handed reel?"

Yes. Several good brands of spinning reels are offered for left-handed casters, the handles being on the right-hand side. A few reels feature handles which are interchangeable from one side to the other. These reversible-handled reels, by the nature of their construction, are not usually as strong and noiseless as the nonreversible type, because the driving gear shaft normally cannot be pinioned to both sides of the gear housing.

If the reader naturally is a left-handed caster with other types of tackle, but has not yet taken up spinning, I should like to make the urgent suggestion that he try to get acquainted with the orthodox method which calls for casting with the right hand and reeling with the left. On several occasions, I have instructed fishermen in spinning who were as left-handed as anyone possibly can be. I insisted that they first try the tackle for right-handed casting, and I am glad to report that these people invariably learned to cast properly with the right hand and never wished to change to the left-handed method. If this can be done, the selection of reels is much larger and the ease and efficiency of spinning is much greater.

Actually, spinning is somewhat of an in-between method, as far as manual operation is concerned. The fly rod fisherman frequently learns to cast with either hand and, if he habitually is a right-handed caster, he must shift the rod to the left hand in order to reel with the right. The plug caster operates similarly. Thus, it is not difficult for either naturally right-handed or naturally left-handed casters to learn the proper spinning method of always using the right hand for casting and the left hand for reeling, without ever changing over.

THE CARE OF SPINNING REELS

The gear housing of a spinning reel is packed with grease. It normally is unnecessary to clean it more often than once every year or two. When this seems advisable, remove the side-plate screws and the side plate, thus exposing the gearing mechanism. (Before doing this, it would be well to remove the reel spool too, so the cup and spindle can be cleaned and so grease will not get on the line.) The gearing mechanism should not be disassembled unless one is sure he knows how to put it back together properly. Sometimes it requires special tools.

Wash the gears and the inside of the housing with gasoline, using a small brush to get all parts clean. Allow the mechanism to dry thoroughly, and then coat all moving parts with a reasonably ample amount of "Lubriplate" or similar reel-lubricating grease, obtainable at any tackle store. Screw the side plate back on securely. This part of the reel now should be ready for many months of additional service without further attention.

In addition, all other moving parts should be lubricated frequently with light machine oil. Many reels have oil holes protected by a sliding latch or by an oiling screw. Expose the holes and add two or three drops of oil to each of them, being sure to reseat the screws tightly. Regardless of whether or not there are oiling holes in the reel, we should lubricate the driving gear shaft (between handle and main gear); the base of the pickup shaft; the spool shaft (or spindle); the brake (on threaded shaft and clutch plate), and the base of the anti-reverse lever. It is well to wipe the entire reel with a cloth to which a small amount of oil has been applied.

This latter step, and as many others as seem advisable, should be taken before the reel is put away after each fishing trip. Nylon lines need not be dried and need no special care other than to keep them clean and free from twisting and abrasion.

If the reel has been used in salt water, the reel spool should be removed and the entire reel should be held under running fresh warm water and then should be dried thoroughly. The use of warm water will aid the reel in drying more quickly. When it is dry, it should be lubricated as above described. If reels are given reasonable care after salt water use, corrosion never should harm them to any extent. I have used several of my reels on salt water, year in and year out, and they still are in perfect condition. It is sensible before going fishing to wipe them with an oily rag and to rub a bit of grease in between the moving parts to keep salt water out.

When the spool is taken off the reel, the inside of

the cup should be wiped clean, as dust is very apt to settle in it and work in between the spindle and its bushing.

FOULING OF LINE BENEATH SPOOL

The base of the spools of several reels is surrounded with a chenille-covered wire which is very similar to a pipe cleaner. This is designed to fill the gap between the cup and the spool to prevent line from dropping between them and thus getting caught in the mechanism beneath. If the chenille becomes worn or matted, it is a simple matter to replace it. The spools of a few reels have a patented "skirt" which covers the cup and which thus entirely prevents line from dropping between cup and spool. This is a most important improvement, because when line does get so caught, in the mechanism beneath the spool, it is almost sure to abrade it as well as being exasperating to the fisherman. The careful angler need never let this happen, but the "skirt" is complete insurance against it. It also helps to keep dirt and spray out of the mechanism.

Regardless of what type of reel one owns, this matter of fouling the line under the spool is very easy to avoid. In rigging the tackle, the anti-reverse mechanism should be engaged, to prevent the reel from backwinding and thus throwing loose coils. In fishing, such an occurrence is due to the angler's failing to keep his line tight. This can be partially prevented by using "forefinger control" of the line, as will be explained in Chapter Eight.

There is another advantage of the skirted type of reel spool (found on the Ru Sport, Ru Mer, Centaure, Ru Atlantic, and a few others) which is fully as important as the points above mentioned. By consulting Figure 5, we note that when a cast is made when

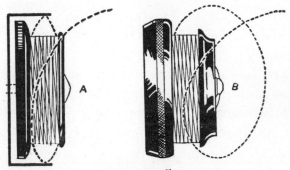

FIGURE 5.

SHOWING (A) HOW UNCOILING LINE IS CHOKED ON CASTS MADE WHEN SPOOL IS RETRACTED INSIDE CUP, AND (B) THE UNIMPEDED UNCOILING OF LINE FROM SPOOLS OF THE "SKIRTED" TYPE

the spool of a reel of the more usual type is retracted into the cup, the uncoiling line slaps against the inside of the cup. This adds enough resistance to cause an appreciable reduction in the distance of the cast. Since, in the "skirted" type of spool, the skirt covers the cup, there is nothing of this nature to impede the uncoiling of the line when making a cast.

NOTES ON PURCHASING A REEL

When we buy a spinning reel it is wise to be sure that replacement parts are available. This is the case with all reels made in this country and with most of those which are imported here. In fact, when a well-known reel becomes damaged, it usually is very easy to get it fixed. Many of the larger spinning tackle specialists keep spare parts in stock and are competent to do repair jobs well and quickly, or to send them to the manufacturer or importer for attention if necessary.

Largely through men in the armed forces, many uncommon reels are being brought to this country from abroad. Some of these are very good ones but others should be avoided, if only for their lack of repair facilities. It is discouraging to buy a nice looking spinning reel and then to discover that we must send it back to Europe to get it fixed!

I have seen several rather unique importations, such as a reel whose pickup swings back and forth instead of revolving with the cup. This does not reverse the twist made in casting and therefore is no better than the outmoded Turn Table reel we learned about earlier. Another one has a spool which is made to wobble, to save the manufacturer the expense of installing a cross-winding mechanism. This is about as sensible as allowing a train to run with wobbling wheels.

I have a beautiful and expensive creation containing an infinite number of needle bearings. I took it apart once, and had lots of the bearings left over. The thing is so complicated that its manufacturer put himself out of business! This may be enough to illustrate my suggestion that, unless we are pretty sure of our ground, it is well to buy well-known and highly regarded reels and to leave the strangers to somebody else.

CHAPTER THREE
Facts about Spinning Lines

WHEN WE READ about spinning, usually it is referred to as a reasonably foolproof method of fishing. "Backlashes are impossible"; "One can learn after only a few minutes of practice"; "Longer casts are easy, and with lighter lures" — these are among the statements which enthusiasts claim for it.

All this is quite true, and yet a surprisingly large percentage of beginners get into trouble with their tackle. Their line may cast off in a snarl of wiry coils. They may have so much slack out that they have difficulty in hooking their fish. The tackle does not cast as far or as easily as it should. Other equally discouraging things happen.

Those who get into such predicaments can take heart from the fact that spinning presents no troubles which cannot be avoided easily. There is a simple remedy for every one; a remedy which it is more sensible to learn before going fishing than when out on the water. Many of these difficulties have to do with the selection of spinning lines and with the way the angler handles them. I hope the following information may make certain that the pleasures and advantages of this sport will be as great as its proponents claim.

What types of spinning lines are available, and what are the differences between them?

Spinning lines all are made from nylon (or from similar materials) because these are mineral fibers and thus do not deteriorate to any extent with age. In earlier years, we had to use lines of Japanese gut, of silk, or of other animal or vegetable fibers, all of which grew weaker and more useless with time. Nylon is a rather complex mineral compound made in this country and abroad under patents controlled by E. I. du Pont de Nemours and Company.[1]

Other somewhat similar substances now are being offered for spinning lines and are being called by other names. Some of these are comparable to nylon in their qualities, while others decidedly are inferior. Certain of these materials are so new that it would be unfair to the product and to the angler to attempt to discuss them. Therefore, let us confine present comments to the various types of nylon lines and let the angler use this as a standard for the evaluation of whatever new developments may come.

Nylon is made of the same elements as those which exist in coal, air and water. It is prepared chemically

---

[1] Du Pont has named its nylon monofilament "Tynex," which now is the registered trade-mark for this product.

in the form of flakes which are fed into machines in which it is melted and from which it is extruded into filaments. These filaments can be drawn out in many sizes, from hairlike ones which are braided into lines of various strengths to the larger single filaments which are complete lines in themselves.

When nylon is made into spinning lines, these can be divided into four rather distinct types; braided multifilament, braided monofilament, American monofilament and French monofilament. It seems rather pointless to delve into too many technical details about these types of lines. There are, however, several facts about each which should be explained because they are of great value to the spinning angler in aiding him to select the proper type for specific fishing purposes.

BRAIDED MULTIFILAMENT

This is very much like the familiar plug or bait casting lines, except that it is made in smaller diameters and strengths for spinning and, unlike plug casting lines, it usually is braided without a core. When it is made with a core (of several twisted threads), the outer sleeve of the line is braided around the core, thus making the line attractively round. When it is made without a core (called "square-braid," "flat-braid," or "solid braid") it looks nearly square in cross section when new, but in use it tends to flatten to a very narrow oval ribbon. The core (if any) and the sleeve are made of threads twisted from many strands of gossamer nylon filaments. Many hundreds of these are used in a single line, thus giving rise to the name "multifilament."

Braided lines for spinning should be made without a core because the core, while contributing to the roundness of the line, adds insufficiently to its strength in proportion to its diameter. The sleeve has a tendency to slip and slide along the core, detracting from the smoothness and casting ability of the line. The core frequently breaks and separates, thus causing a weak section which interferes with good casting.

Braided lines made without a core have nothing to support their roundness and therefore tend to be flat. This is advantageous in that more line can be packed on the spool. The flatness visibly signals to the angler when the line is becoming twisted. Coreless lines afford greater strength for their diameters and are more stable in strength because there is no core to give way under strain.

All braided lines are woven with greater or lesser degrees of tightness, depending on the closeness of the crisscrossing of the threads. Those braided tightly are called "hard-braided," while those braided loosely are termed "soft-braided" lines. Manufacturers attempt to strike a happy medium in making spinning lines by braiding them hard enough to make them relatively stiff and strong and yet not so hard-braided that the strands will cut each other under tension.

If the braiding of these lines should be examined

under a magnifying glass, we would see an interweaving of the threads which looks like the weaving of a basket. Thus, there are spaces between the braids into which water may be absorbed, making the line waterlogged. This would harm its casting qualities by adding weight, by making the coils stick to each other and by making the wet line cling to the rod in casting. To prevent this, manufacturers waterproof their lines in one way or another to fill up the spaces between the filaments, thus keeping the line relatively dry. This waterproofing is not entirely permanent and it is impractical for the angler to attempt to renew it.

Another reason for waterproofing is to add stiffness, which materially improves casting. Lines which are insufficiently stiff cast like wet string, operating poorly because they cling to the rod when they slap against it and because the soft, wet coils also cling to each other. The degree of stiffness is important, therefore, in selecting a line. The line should be as stiff as possible without setting in hard coils. In deciding upon the degree of stiffness desirable, we should take into account that the line will be much more supple when wet and also that use will add to its pliability as the waterproofing becomes worn from the surface.

Braided multifilament lines can be obtained in black, white, gray and in many other tones, including multicolored lines. I agree with many experienced fishermen who have learned that color makes little or no difference. All such lines are opaque, and thus, when viewed from below by the fish, they appear nearly equally dark, regardless of their color. But if the fish have no preference, the anglers usually have. Some like a white line because they can see it more easily, aiding them in locating the lure. Others like a darker color because they have the impression that it seems less visible. We may as well select the color that strikes our fancy. Evidently the matter is of small importance to the fish.

BRAIDED MONOFILAMENT

A relatively few manufacturers have made available ranges of sizes in braided monofilament lines which, as the name implies, are woven from nylon monofilaments instead of from nylon threads. Thus, instead of there being many hundred tiny filaments twisted and braided together as in braided multifilament lines, the braided monofilaments consist of relatively few, but much larger, single nylon strands; usually eight or twelve or a multiple of four, made either with or without a core. The majority of these lines are not waterproofed and do not need to be, because the larger filaments are much stiffer and not so absorptive of water. Manufacturers boast of secret processes for treating these lines to improve them in various ways but, when all is said and done, there seems to be little difference between them.

I like this type of line because, in general, it is ideally stiff and because it does not lose its stiffness with use. These lines cast beautifully and can be depended upon for strength. But since most of them are in the larger diameters, they are more suitable for salt water than for fresh water fishing. The necessarily hard braid of the relatively small number of strong filaments makes the untreated lines rather abrasive against rod guides and even against the rods themselves. If these lines were treated to prevent abrasion completely, it would seem that there would be little difference between them and nylon monofilament. In any event, as this is written, the tendency of these lines to cut into (or to score) rod guides must be considered a disadvantage.

AMERICAN MONOFILAMENT

This popular type of line is extruded in a single filament which makes the entire line, in effect, a leader. All nylon monofilament is made by the du Pont company, which sells it to line manufacturers who dye and respool it on their own line spools in the accepted lengths for use on spinning reels. In this respect, American nylon monofilament is American nylon monofilament, no matter who sells it or by what name it is called. Some of the converters (the line manufacturers) state that they use secret processes for improving it in one way or another. It is probable that some of this is true but, in general, it would appear that if important methods for improvements were known and were feasible, the extensive and ultra-efficient du Pont laboratories would have developed and adopted them in the first place.

Nylon monofilament absorbs about 7 per cent of water and therefore becomes more pliable when wet. It is produced for spinning in strengths of from less than two pounds test to those far above the spinning range, and in a wide choice of colors. It requires no leader, since it is a leader in itself. Being translucent, it is less noticeable to fish than are braided lines. It can be depended upon for strength.

In 1952, the du Pont company introduced an improved monofilament called "Type 4," made especially for use in fishing lines. This is about 35 per cent stronger than the old nylon, and about 25 per cent limper — or very similar to French nylon in strength and suppleness.

FRENCH MONOFILAMENT

Although French and American nylon are made under the same patents, anglers who have tried both kinds often feel that French nylon seems more pliable and easier to use. If this is so, probably it is because the French manufacturers of tackle have been studying its adaptation for fishing longer than we have. To me, there seems to be very little difference between the two except, perhaps, in the matter of resiliency, or "comeback."

When we get "hung up" and have to break loose, or when we are handling a very strong fish, nylon

monofilament has a valuable safety factor of being able
to stretch. In both American and foreign nylon, the
factor of stretch has been adjusted to an ideal degree;
enough for safety, but not so much as to impede the
hooking and handling of fish. A reasonable amount of
stretch is important in taking up the shock of a strike
or of a sudden run, particularly when using very fine
lines.

When nylon is stretched under such circumstances,
it gradually recovers to approach its former length.
This recovery of stretch takes place to a greater extent
in some monofilaments than in others, but never entirely in any. As a result, constant use of a line gradually makes it longer and longer, and therefore weaker
and weaker. After using a great many lines over a great
many years, it is my impression that the resiliency of
French monofilament is somewhat superior to that of
the American. I would urge, however, that anglers
try both types to decide this question for themselves.
In any event, the gradual deterioration of nylon monofilaments due to failure to recover stretch entirely
makes it advisable to test old lines occasionally *when
thoroughly wet* to decide how much of their strength
they have lost. I have stressed the words "when thoroughly wet" because weakness shows up more when a
line is wet than when it is dry.

Nylon monofilament does not grow weak with age,
when left wet or dry on the reel spool, but it does
grow weak from stretching due to continued use. For-

tunately it is low in cost, and it seems very sensible to replace old lines with new ones from time to time, especially before going where large fish are in prospect.

The matter of color is, as we have noted, more important to the angler than to the fish. Any unobtrusive color, such as gray, pale green, or gray-green, will do nicely. It is well to be sure that the line has

Line Size	Pounds Test	Diameter in Mms	Diameter in Inches
*E[1]	1.25	10/100	.0039
*F	1.50	12/100	.0047
*H	1.75	14/100	.0055
†L[2]	2.20	16/100	.0063
†M	2.64	18/100	.0071
†N	3.08	20/100	.0079
†O	3.33	22/100	.0087
†P	4.40	24/100	.0095
Q	5.17	26/100	.0103
R	5.94	28/100	.0110
S	6.60	30/100	.0118
T	7.26	32/100	.0126
V	8.36	35/100	.0138
Y	10.56	40/100	.0158
Z	12.76	45/100	.0177
ZZ	15.40	50/100	.0197

[1] Sizes marked * are obtainable on 50-meter (55 yd.) spools only.

[2] Sizes marked † are available on both 50-meter and 110-yard spools. Others are on 110-yard spools only.

been dyed or treated to remove all shine and glint, so that it will not reflect sunlight.

In European countries, French brands of monofilament, such as Mitchell, Water Queen and Tortue, are used almost exclusively, while braided nylon is used practically not at all. The French have gone in for extremely light casting and therefore have developed an amazing range of sizes. An example of this is the popular brand called Tortue, which is sold widely in this country and which offers sizes shown on page 60.

As a means of comparison with the table opposite, the following gives standard American monofilament sizes and strengths:

Pounds Test	Comparable Tippet Size	Diameter in Inches	Tolerance in Inches Plus or Minus
1.25	5X	.006	.0005
1.75	4X	.007	.0005
2.25	3X	.008	.0005
2.9	2X	.009	.0005
3.5	1X	.010	.0005
4.3	0X	.011	.0005
5.1	9/5	.012	.0005
6.0	8/5	.013	.001
7.0	7/5	.014	.001
8.0	6/5	.015	.001
9.1	5/5	.016	.001
10.3	4/5	.017	.001
11.5	3/5	.018	.0015
12.8	2/5	.019	.0015
15.6	0/5	.021	.0015

OTHER MONOFILAMENTS

New monofilaments, similar to nylon, are appearing for use as spinning lines. These, made principally in Germany, are publicized as being stronger for their diameters than is nylon. If this is true, the difference seems to be very minor. I have used several of these brands and agree with other anglers that they are not yet superior to nylon. Their principal fault, which later may be corrected, is that they fatigue under tension, becoming crinkly like a pulled hair, which is a decided disadvantage in use. They do not "come back" as much after stretching as does nylon, and thus they more quickly lose their resiliency, having an inadequate reserve of stretch to act as a shock absorber in striking or in playing a fish.

NOTES ON SELECTING LINES

If one were to take a straw vote on the types of lines preferred by spinning anglers, it might work out something like this: Beginners would find braided multifilament easier to use since it is limper than monofilament and causes less trouble with twisting and improper spooling. They would find all types of monofilament advantageous because no leaders are necessary. Anglers generally would find braided lines of advantage in fishing floating bass bugs and plugs which require manipulation, because the softer and more clinging braided lines spool better under lack

of tension. They would find braided lines excellent for
live bait fishing for the same reason, although more
experienced fishermen would prefer monofilament because of its lesser visibility. Experienced anglers would
prefer French or American monofilament for nearly
all purposes because of its ideal combination of suppleness, smoothness and lack of visibility. All anglers
would prefer braided lines or French monofilament in
tests of six pounds or more because the slightly greater
stiffness of American monofilament grows relatively
more pronounced as the diameters become greater.

Incidentally, those who enjoy fly-fishing will find
the wide range of American and French monofilament
sizes ideal for tying tapered leaders. In the smaller
sizes, the French fifty-five-yard spools are little larger
in diameter than a half dollar and so several of them
can be carried conveniently in the pocket. These spools
in the Tortue brand come in plastic dispensers which
allow any length to be unrolled as needed without
damage to the rest. Since using monofilament for fly
rod leaders and tippets I have found it equal in every
way to the best silkworm gut, with the added advantage that it does not need soaking. As a result, my
silkworm gut leaders have been neglected in recent
years, even for use with the dry fly.

Knowing this about spinning lines should be of
value, though understanding how to spool them and
how to use them properly is of much greater importance. Much of how to use them will be taken up in

Chapter Eight in discussing casting, but here it seems pertinent to deal more with the preparation of the tackle than with its use.

SPOOLING LINES

When lines are transferred from the spools on which they are purchased to the reel spools on which they are to be used, it is important to put them on with as little twisting as possible, and especially to do so under reasonable tension, properly cross-wound, in order to enjoy trouble-free, efficient long-distance casting.

HOW TO PUT LINES ON REEL SPOOLS

A great deal of what has been written about putting lines on reel spools seems to be needlessly complicated when, in fact, the procedure is extremely simple, even though it takes a bit of time. Here are two of the easiest and most popular methods.

INDOOR METHOD

Unfasten the end of the line and tie a Perfection Loop knot in it. Place the line spool over a convenient nail or something similar, as shown in Figure 6, so that the line will unroll from the revolving spool, rather than uncoiling from a nonrevolving one. If two or more connected spools are to be used, fasten them temporarily together by sticking Scotch tape around the adjoining rims so they will revolve together and thus not tangle or damage the line. Make a slip noose with the loop knot and slip it over the reel spool (which has been removed from the reel). If the line is pulled back against the loop, it will tighten itself on the hub of the

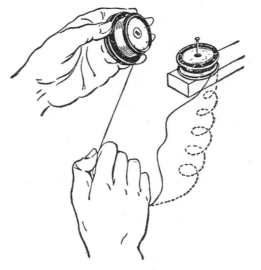

FIGURE 6.

A METHOD OF TRANSFERRING LINE FROM A
LINE SPOOL TO A REEL SPOOL

*Line spool should revolve when paying out line. Wind
line (clockwise on most reels) with even tension. Reverse
reel spool in left hand whenever twist (dotted line)
appears.*

reel spool and will be securely fastened into place. Most reels demand that the line be wound on clockwise (an exception being the Mitchell reel, which goes counter-clockwise); so let's take a few turns in this direction to be sure the line is started right.

Now, holding the reel spool as shown in the sketch, wind on the line under sufficient tension to insure that each coil is firmly seated under slight stretch so that it will not become loose. In doing this, a certain amount of care is needed to wind on the line evenly, without leaving gaps or valleys, and without piling too much on one side or the other.

After a dozen or so turns have been made, it may be noticed that the line between winding hand and line spool is setting in coils. When these coils become pronounced, face the reel spool in the opposite direction and continue winding. Then the coils will disappear and later begin to set themselves up in the reverse direction. Each time this happens, merely reverse the reel spool in the hand to get rid of them. This regular reversal in winding neutralizes the tendency to twist and, if a fairly equal number of turns arc taken before each reversal of the reel spool, the line can be put on it with almost no twist at all. Very slight twist is unavoidable and unimportant. It is only excessive twist that gets the angler into difficulty.

The correct amount of line which should be put on a reel spool is shown in Figure 7. It is important to fill the spool to the lip only and not to pack on all the line it possibly can hold. An overfilled spool will cause the line to drop off of its own accord, and the resulting tangles will be a nuisance and a hazard to casting. This is more true of monofilament than of braided nylon; one can safely put on a bit more of the latter than of the former. An underfilled spool penalizes the angler in the distance he can cast because the line must slide farther up over the lip of the spool, thus causing unnecessary drag or friction.

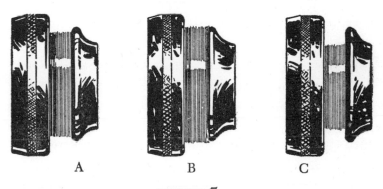

A   B   C

FIGURE 7.

PROPERLY AND IMPROPERLY FILLED REEL
SPOOLS

*Spool A is properly filled to lip only. Spool B is overfilled.
Spool C is underfilled.*

In the above method it will be noted that the line has not been cross-wound to any extent. This partially will be taken care of in fishing by making a short cast and then a few increasingly longer ones. When the opportunity permits, it is well to cross-wind the entire line so that it will pay out smoothly when a fish is taking out more than normal of the reserve. This can be done from a slowly moving boat on a lake or large river by letting out all of the line and then by reeling it in under proper tension. It also can be done on dry land where a very long lawn or a roadway or sidewalk is available, as will be explained in the next method.

Outdoor Method

This way of spooling the line is popular in France and it seems to me to be the most practical and probably the easiest. Run the line from the line spool through the guides of a rod, from tip-top to butt guide, and fasten the end of the line to the reel spool as before. Slide the line spool (or spools) over a pencil and have someone hold them at a distance of twenty feet or so away, allowing the spools to unroll under mild tension while the angler reels the line from the line spool onto the reel by turning the handle of the reel. In doing this, the line will be cross-wound, but there will be a mild twist in it. To remove this twist, have someone pull out all of the line and lay it straight out on the ground in a spot where it will be free from catching on twigs and from dirt. A lawn obviously is the best place for this, if a long enough clear space can be found.

Now, hold the line between thumb and forefinger near the butt guide of the rod and reel it in, allowing the line to slide between thumb and forefinger under proper tension. This will stroke out nearly all of the twist and will install the line on the reel properly.

Both of these methods take a bit of time but, once done, the line need not be removed except to reverse it or replace it. Nylon lines can be left on the reel spool year in and year out without harm, since they will not deteriorate, even when put away wet.

It is handy to have a means of keeping the line tightly on the spool so that it will not uncoil when not in use. Several of the newer reels have line clips installed on their reel spools for this purpose. If the reel does not have one, merely tie a knot in one end of a wide rubber band and slip the band over the line on the spool. The knot provides a tab which allows the band to be removed easily. It is possible to buy line clips (like bicycle trouser-leg guards) for this purpose, but the rubber band saves this cost and it takes up less room when the reel is being used.

EXTRA REEL SPOOLS

Nearly all reels are sold with but a single spool, but additional reel spools can be purchased when the reel is bought, or later on. The spools of most reels can be changed in a matter of seconds to give the angler as much of a variety in choices of lines as he has spools for them. I know men who carry four or more extra spools, each filled with line of one make or size, or another. I should like to recommend that all spinning anglers carry at least one extra spool, partly to provide another line in case a long length of the first becomes broken and lost. Many fishermen use braided and monofilament lines alternately, depending on fishing requirements, and many like a choice of strengths, knowing that they can cast farther with the lighter line but that the heavier one may be more useful when fishing near obstructions.

METHOD OF IDENTIFYING LINES

When a line is bought, it is useful to remember its size, make, and other data about it; particularly when the line is one of several. I don't like to scratch identifying marks on the spool itself because this mars the appearance of the reel and because the line probably will be changed later anyway. It seems handiest to type or print this data on a tiny piece of paper and to stick it to the spool with Scotch tape. If we buy two spools of Cortland six-pound monofilament, for example, and have half a spool remaining after putting the line on the reel spool, we have used about one hundred and fifty yards. The symbol therefore might read "150-6#C." Most anglers have their own systems of symbols and any will do as long as it can be remembered. It is a good idea to mark an old or slightly abraded line with a danger symbol so that it will be used only as a spare and not when we need every ounce of reserve in trying for a big fish. It is remarkable how easily lines can get mixed up, or the information about them forgotten, if such a means of identification is not used. The little label can be stuck on the underside of the spool where it will not come into contact with moving parts. In this place it is not noticeable and it is protected from being rubbed off.

Lines for spinning are relatively inexpensive, and a more than normally ample reserve is good insurance in case of a break or of an unusually long run of some fish. Therefore, I like to fill my spools completely with line to the exclusion of backing. I buy either two or three connected (if possible) spools to get a more than ample amount and I fill the reel spool with it, saving the remainder for use for splicing later, when enough of the terminal end has been removed to make this necessary. A full spool rarely is needed, although I can remember occasions when I required all of it; one, when the full two hundred yards was not enough to stop the fish! This reserve, however, allows the line to be reversed on the spool when necessary, so it is a doubly sensible procedure.

SPLICING LINES

It should be noted that the Barrel Knot is recommended for splicing lines. I know of no other knot so suitable. The knot should be tested carefully after being tied, as occasionally it draws together improperly, allowing the cross-pull on the strands to cut them. When tied correctly, this knot is nearly as strong as the line itself. It slips easily through the guides and, if the ends have been cut off closely, it does not catch in coming off the reel. I have found it very satisfactory also in tying a monofilament leader to a braided line. In this case, it is preferable to use a leader of the same strength as the line. Of course, continuous lines are preferable to spliced ones, but a spliced line is a very minor disadvantage and the situation frequently cannot be avoided.

AVOIDING AND REMOVING LINE TWIST

The experienced spinning angler never should be troubled with twisted lines because it is so easy to avoid them. Sometimes, line twist is caused by using lures that rotate in the water. Most of the good lures do not rotate and, except in special cases, I am inclined to discard those that do, because they are somewhat of a nuisance. If we want to keep lures that have a tendency to twist the line, notice whether they twist to the right or to the left and mark them accordingly by scratching an "R" or an "L" on them. Keep the "right twisters" in one place, the "left twisters" in another, and the "nontwisters" somewhere else in the tackle box. If it is noticed that a twist is appearing in the line, merely change the lure to one which revolves in the opposite direction until the twist is removed.

Troubles with twisted lines also occur when spinning tackle is used in trolling, since most baits and lures will spin to a certain extent if the boat is moving fast enough. This will get a fisherman into difficulty if he does not take a simple step to avoid it. Obtain a few of the plastic or metal keels shown in Chapter Five, Figures 26 and 27, and fasten one to the line (or between line and leader) a few feet ahead of the lure. Swivels alone do very little good because, under tension, most of them do not "swiv." The combination of two swivels and a keel is ideal, and the choice between keels of plastic or of metal (usually lead) depends upon whether we wish to troll the lure near the surface or at a distance below it, or whether or not we need the added weight in casting. The size of the keel should be proportionate to the size or intensity of spin of the lure, since a tiny keel used with a large lure may not be sufficiently effective. Chapter Five tells how keels can be made.

In my earlier days of spinning I learned the value of keels the hard way. I had been trolling for an hour or so with a long monofilament line out, when I suddenly noticed that the line was beginning to twist near the rod tip. By that time, the tackle certainly was a mess. I managed to pull the line in by hand until I reached the terminal end, at the same time letting the rest trail behind the boat in a long U. Trying to stroke out the twist did little good, and would have taken much too long anyway. However, it was easy to determine the direction of the twist and to put on a fast revolving lure which would spin in the opposite direction. I let ten or fifteen feet of line out and held it in my fingers to be sure that the lure was removing the twist instead of making it worse.

The lure rapidly untwisted the line and, as I let it out a few feet at a time to avoid tangles, everything soon was put to rights again.

Usually, a line which is not badly twisted can be straightened by taking off the lure and by trolling the line behind a boat, or in the current downstream. Slight twists can be stroked out by hand, beginning near the terminal end and working backward. When all is said and done, twisted lines are the fault of the angler, who never should have allowed this to happen in the first place.

By far the most common cause of line twist is the tendency of the angler to crank his reel against a slipping clutch while not recovering line. Every time the reel handle is turned, under such circumstances, the only result is to put several twists in the line for every turn of the handle. Therefore, we cannot stress too strongly that the handle should not be turned if inadequate brake tension allows the spool to rotate, showing that line is not being recovered.

"But," someone says, "what should we do when we have a big fish on and we cannot recover line, even though the brake is set as tight as we dare to set it?"

The answer to this is to "pump in" the fish, as will be discussed in more detail later. With the rod low, and the line tight, place the forefinger of the rod hand against the reel spool to keep it from turning. Raise the rod tip gradually to the vertical, and reel in the slack as the rod tip is lowered. When the line thus obtained is reeled in, merely repeat the process as often as necessary. The pressure of the forefinger on the reel spool is enough to allow this, but not so much as to prevent the fish from making a run if he chooses to do so. This forefinger pressure on the reel spool provides an excellent and instantaneous auxiliary brake, of which more will be said later.

REMOVING WIRINESS

Some monofilament lines may be too wiry for efficient casting unless they are limbered up. They usually become supple after a few casts, but we may prefer to make them so before fishing. To do this, rig the tackle and hook the lure to a convenient tree or bush. Then walk away with the rod, paying out the castable length of line, or a little more. When this is done, grip the reel spool firmly and, with the rod pointed at the lure, pull the line enough to remove the wiriness. Then reel it in again under proper tension. This can be done easily and quickly, and at the same time it serves to test the strength of the line. It is not necessary with most of the monofilaments, but is helpful when needed.

FOUR IMPORTANT KNOTS AND HOW TO TIE THEM

Suitable knots, correctly tied, are important in all types of fishing. In spinning, they are even more so because of the extremely light and fine lines which commonly are used. In all fresh water spinning there are but four knots which are very important, but these four are of such great value that every fisherman should learn to tie them quickly and well. Each one has its place in spinning and I have never known any of them to pull loose, once correctly tied.

Contrary to the beliefs of some fishermen, it is easy to tie knots with nylon and it is easy to make them hold securely. Two things should be remembered, in addition to knowing how to tie the knot: First, pull it tight slowly, rather than with a jerk. And remember to pull it *tight*! Second, always test the knot. It may go together improperly and thus be weak. Give it as strong a pull as seems reasonable. If it holds, it is almost sure to be tied correctly.

The four important knots are:

The Perfection Loop Knot — for fastening the line to the reel spool, for quickly changing lures, for use with the plastic ball float and for other purposes.

The Barrel Knot — for splicing lines, for making droppers, and for tying leaders to lines.

The Clinch Knot — for tying to the line or leader swivels, snap swivels, floats or ringed eyed lures (that is, lures with eyes turned neither up nor down).

The Turle Knot — for tying to the line or leader any lure which has a turned up or turned down eye.

It has always seemed difficult for me to learn to tie

a knot by looking at a diagram; so in learning I have asked other anglers to demonstrate it. These four knots are not difficult to learn.

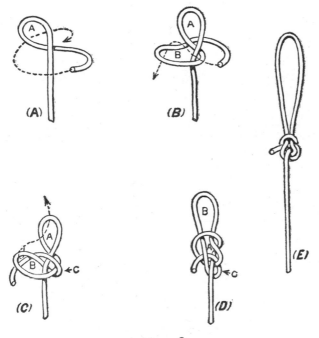

FIGURE 8.

THE PERFECTION LOOP KNOT

The Perfection Loop Knot: This is used also in tying the loop on the snell of a hook or fly and in making the loop on a fly rod leader. Throw a loop as shown in A, Figure 8, holding the crossing between thumb and forefinger. Throw a second loop around the crossing as shown in B, and bring the end around again between the two turns as shown in C. Now, push the second loop (B) through the first loop (A) and pull on both loop and leader until the loop jams as shown in D. The finished knot should look like E. We can make this loop as large or as small as we wish. If it is tied correctly, the end will stick out from the knot at right angles to the line. It can be snipped off closely with finger-nail clippers.

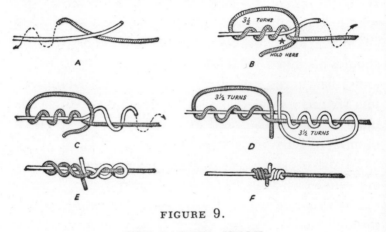

FIGURE 9.

THE BARREL KNOT

The Barrel Knot: Lap the ends of the two strands to be joined by forming an "X" with the ends about three inches long, as shown in Figure 9. Twist one short end around the other strand six times, as shown in Figure 9, A, and then bring the short end between the other short end and the other strand. Hold it there with thumb and forefinger. Now wind the other short end around the other strand six times as shown in B,

but in the *opposite* direction from the way the first
turns were made. Push the short end through the loop
in which the first end is inserted, but in the *opposite*
direction, as shown in C. Now, pull slowly on both
lines, being sure the short ends you have inserted do
not come out. The knot now will look like D. As it is
pulled tight, the turns will gather and draw closer
(as in E) until the knot looks like F. That's all there
is to it, except to snip off the short ends closely
with finger-nail clippers.

On this knot, opinions vary as to how many turns
should be taken. The illustrations show only three-
and-a-half turns for simplicity's sake. In joining nylon, six turns seem to be ideally strong, although one
more or less can be tried as long as there is an equal
number of turns on both sides.

To make a *dropper*, with this knot, merely leave
one end much longer and don't cut it off.

The Clinch Knot: This is an easy one! Stick the end
through the eye of the lure (or swivel) about three
inches and wind it around the line six or seven times.
Now, push the line end through the loop between the
eye and the coils as shown in A. Pull on the lure and
line, being sure that the line end does not pull out.
The coils will settle as shown in B when the knot is
pulled tight. Be sure to pull it tight, and then snip
off the end as closely as possible to the knot.

Many fishermen consider the Improved Clinch Knot
(Figure 10 A, B) superior to the Clinch Knot. It is

tied in the same way, except that the end shown in A is then passed through the upper loop and jammed tight in this position.

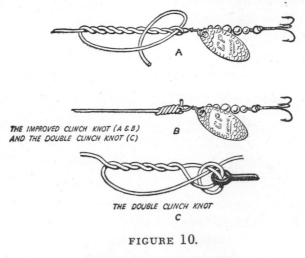

A

THE IMPROVED CLINCH KNOT (A & B)
AND THE DOUBLE CLINCH KNOT (C)   B

THE DOUBLE CLINCH KNOT
C

FIGURE 10.

THE CLINCH KNOT

Other anglers carry this a step farther, as shown in the Double Clinch Knot (Figure 10 C), and they recommend it especially when using heavy monofilament. Run a second loop through the first loop and through the eye of the hook, and then twist the loose end three times around the stem. Then, return the end through the extra loop next to the eye of the hook and tighten the knot.

I never have had trouble with the simple Clinch Knot, and have used it habitually, but so many fishermen seem to prefer one or the other of the above variations that it seems advisable to include them.

The Turle Knot: This is widely used in fly-fishing, but less so in spinning because the latter calls for fewer lures with turned-up or turned-down eyes. Run the end of the line through the eye of the lure as shown in Figure 11, and, with the lure thus strung on

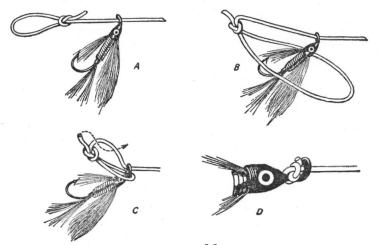

FIGURE 11.

THE TURLE KNOT

the line, forget it temporarily. Make a "single running" knot in the end (some call it a "slip-noose") and pull it tight as shown in A. Slip the loop over the lure and place the loop around the turned up or turned down eye, as in B. With the loop tight against the neck of the lure (as in C), pull the line until the knot is tight *around* the eye of the lure, making it look like D. Cut off the excess end, and the knot is done. To make this knot doubly secure, tie a regular knot in the end of the line just above the single running knot and work it in close, then cutting off the excess.

I should like to stress the value, in spinning, of these little finger-nail clippers. They are indispensable in cutting knot ends closely and in cutting off lures. Nearly all drug and sporting-goods stores carry them.

It seems proper to repeat that a basic requirement in spinning is the use of the light line. This, of course, is a relative term, depending on what tackle we are using, where we are fishing, and what we are fishing for. The common tendency is to use lines much heavier or stronger than necessary. We can cast farther and easier with light lines than with heavier ones. Light lines bring better luck because they are less noticeable to the fish. So it always is a good rule to use the lightest ones advisable under the circumstances. Beginners in spinning are amazed to discover how strong even lines of two or three pounds in test actually are! When we get hung up and have to break our lure loose, this valuable point becomes even more firmly embedded in mind. Light lines add up to longer, more delicate casts, to catching more fish, and to having more fun fishing. There is an ideal range of sizes of lines to suit each rod and there is an ideal range of weights of lures to suit each line. Matching the various elements of tackle properly together in weight, strength, or size pays valuable dividends in getting better results from spinning.

We shall go into greater detail later about the great importance of keeping spinning lines wound tightly on reel spools. It will suffice here to say that this requires that the angler always must reel in under tension to keep loose loops from forming on the spool. Slack must be eliminated in the line and on the reel at all times if one is to control his casts, his fish, and is to keep clear of difficulties with his tackle.

CHAPTER FOUR

Choices and Uses of Spinning Lures

I SOMETIMES WONDER whether or not a fisherman selecting lures in a tackle shop has more difficulty making decisions than a kid in a candy store. The choices among the hundreds of lures available certainly makes decision seem equally difficult — at least until the fisherman realizes that a few well-chosen ones will do as well as many picked at random.

For years I collected spinning lures and faithfully tried almost everything new that came out. I carried them in boxes stuffed into my fishing jacket, and the horde accumulated until I was afraid of becoming rather dangerously top-heavy. I feared to part with any one of them, because that one might be the secret weapon that would save the day!

Suddenly it occurred to me that the majority of those I carried were relatively unproductive, and that a few favorites did their work admirably well under almost all conditions. I picked out these most successful ones, and found that they were confined to only three or four of a type: a few spinners with individual characteristics; some wobblers or spoons of various shapes, sizes and weights; a weighted fly or two, and a dozen or so small plugs divided between surface, diving and deep-running actions.

Right then and there I weeded out my inconsequential lures and fitted up a small tackle box with examples only of the more successful types. The few proved to be as productive as the many, and streamside selection was made quick and easy. Season by season I add a new one or two and retire an equal number of lesser value. No longer does the vast collection in a tackle store perplex me, because I have learned that lures should be chosen and used according to the dictates of weather, of water conditions, of the necessary length of the cast, and of the estimated desires of the type of fish being sought at the moment, rather than by arbitrarily grasping at any pretty trinket that strikes one's fancy, regardless of its action or purpose.

For every good lure in the average tackle store there are many which are of little value. The wise buyer must learn to separate the wheat from the chaff. Many lures are created as the result of years of painstaking trial and error by anglers who knew what they were doing and who had a definite purpose in mind. Others merely have evolved from someone's mercenary pipe dream; made only to sell, and destined to be passed over by anglers who know their fishing.

Charles Helin, for example, spent years developing the Flatfish, considered by many to be the most productive plug ever conceived. He labored long and lovingly to reach its perfection of action and balance. This plug has the reputation of having been imitated more often than any other in existence, yet hundreds of thousands of fishermen still seek out the famous original.

A gentleman in France invented the C. P. Swing, perhaps the most famous and most productive of the spinners from an international standpoint. He made the lure heavy enough to cast with spinning tackle, yet light enough to hold its position in a moderate current, even in shallow water, without catching on the bottom. The long, thin blade was designed to spin quickly and efficiently. I know of no fresh water game fish which will not take the C. P. Swing at least as often, on the average, as any other lure. One can find many imitations that resemble it, but I never have seen one that could induce the amazing results of the original.

Some years ago it occurred to me that a wobbler might be devised with a more erratic action than those I had been using. I hate to think of the scores of carefully developed patterns that went into the trash basket before the Birdwing wobbler and spinner finally evolved. The result, shaped like a bird's wing, is irregular and yet so balanced that it will not twist a line. The unusual shape reacts instantly to the slightest motion of current or rod, producing a darting, fluttering action that seems to draw fish from afar.

The carefully developed Dardevle is a balanced

wobbler whose fame is such that no fisherman in his right mind would fail to carry and to use a few, particularly in the one-fifth-ounce size so well adapted to medium power spinning. The Dardevle is fairly expensive, and there are many cheap imitations. Yet the original usually is preferred by fishermen who want the best.

The same is true of many other lures. There is a fascinating story behind the development of each one. It is unfortunate that space does not permit relating some of them, because each story would indicate anew that good lures are expertly designed as the result of infinite labor. They rarely happen by chance, as the uninitiated angler might presume.

Spinning lures, as we have seen, come within the weight range suitable to the tackle being used. In this range we need a few of each type, selected for variance of action, for casting qualities, for suitable depth of operation, and for the amount of their light reflection. Let's discuss each type in turn and see what will suffice.

SPINNERS

A few good spinners and a few good wobblers are the basis of every well-chosen lure assortment. They are so important that many experienced anglers say, "Give me some efficient ones of both types and I won't need anything else." What do they mean by "efficient"?

An efficient spinner is one whose blade revolves easily under the slightest pull of current or rod. It is one whose body does not revolve and thus twist the line. It is one which casts to reasonable or desirable distances; this depending upon its combination of weight and lack of wind-resistance. Of course it is one so designed that its action in the water will be attractive to fish.

A spinner too light for the power of the tackle can be made to cast farther by adding a few split shot to the line a foot or so above the lure. This also makes the lure fish deeper, a quality which often is desirable. If the spinner tends to twist the line (which it may do in a fast current but not in a slow one), this can be overcome by adding one of the various types of keels described in the next chapter.

There are many types of spinner blades, a few of the most important of which are shown in Figure 12. For the most part, the difference between them is minor, insofar as catching fish is concerned. A minimum assortment of spinning blade lures should include one or two with a long, narrow blade and one or two short, wide-bladed lures. Long, slim-bladed spinners will revolve closer to the shank of the lure than the shorter and wider ones; the two divergent types providing a maximum variety of action. Non-symmetrical blades, such as the Kidney and the Birdwing, offer more erratic, fluttering motion and thus are valuable as a third alternative.

FIGURE 4

WILLOW LEAF

KIDNEY

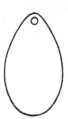

INDIANA

COLORADO

JUNE BUG

ABU

BIRDWING

FLUTED

C. P. SWING

MONTREAL

RED

VIREX

PROPELLER

TRIFACE

HARDY

FIGURE 12.

TYPICAL SPINNER BLADES

Even more important than the design or shape of the spinner is the matter of its size. This usually is dictated by the type of water being fished. A large-bladed spinner will not twist a line when used in quiet waters, but it may twist it badly in the rapids of a swiftly moving stream. A large-bladed spinner, particularly a very shiny one, may present too much flash on bright days, but may be just the thing to use on a dull day or when the water is discolored.

As an example of this: Once I wanted to watch the effect of various lures upon trout. I sat quietly upon a high ledge overlooking a pool, while my partner stood at the head of the pool and let his lure swing with the current to cover the positions of the fish, which I could see clearly. On his first cast he used a large, bright spinner. I could follow it easily as it flashed in an arc, carried by the current to where the fish were feeding. When it came into their vision, every trout scooted for cover, obviously disturbed by the brightness and unnaturalness of the lure. The angler rested the pool and soon the trout resumed their positions again. This time the fisherman put on his smallest and dullest spinner. When this one came to the fish, a large trout went for it and took it. The angler netted three sizable fish with this lure and then, as an experiment, tried a different bright one, which caused the fish to take cover as before.

Many such experiences as this indicate that spinning anglers should have small and dull spinning lures for bright days and clear water and should have larger, brighter ones for overcast days or for times when waters are high and discolored. Under these latter conditions, a fish may not see the spinner at all unless it is large and shiny enough to be visible from a distance in the murky water. In addition, the size of the spinner and that of its hook must be suitable to the size of the fish. I have seen many fishermen using large spinners on small streams where most of the fish were not much bigger than the lure! Some spinners repel fish under certain conditions. Some do not interest them and others attract them. When the wrong one is used, it serves to turn what could have been a productive day into a relatively fishless one. Big spinners may do for big waters, but small streams and ponds containing small fish call for ones more tiny.

Of all the colors, brass or copper usually is most popular for fresh water, just as a silver-colored finish is better for salt. Many spinners are equipped with painted blades or with blades of white or colored pearl. These, to my mind, generally are not important acquisitions, although one or two may prove valuable on occasion. Size and brightness seem to be the two vital characteristics. Blades usually are lacquered to preserve their finish. I frequently remove the lacquer from one side of the blade by scrubbing it with a lacquer solvent; then I allow the blade to tarnish, and possibly later recoat it when it has reached a satisfactory color tone.

In addition to the above, a basic spinner collection should have a few near-surface and a few deep-running types. This is not necessarily a matter of weight, but rather of resistance to the water's current. The C. P. Swing, for example, sinks less readily than a more compactly built spinner such as the Birdwing. The former will hold itself in a mild current without catching bottom, and thus can be worked downstream in and out of the current around rocks and similar good positions. The latter does the same in faster currents and its compact, bulletlike body allows it to sink quickly when allowed to, thus exploring the depths of the waters to greater advantage.

In earlier days, the Devon type of spinner was considered a necessity. It has fallen into disfavor in this country, partly because of the several treble hooks it normally carries, which generally are considered to be both unsportsmanlike and a nuisance. For a time, Devons were sold in pairs, one revolving to the right and one to the left, so that they could be interchanged when the line became twisted. Such difficulties now are unnecessary, especially with the advent of several propeller-type lures which will not twist the line, such as the Proptic spinner shown in the illustration of "Typical Spinners and Wobblers."

Some spinners are equipped with rigidly attached hooks and some with loose hooks. With the rigid hook type, the hook is less inclined to double back and foul itself on the line. This type is less suitable for fish which habitually jump and shake because its rigid construction offers greater opportunity for the fish to throw the lure. If the hook fouls the line, it may be made semirigid by slipping a short piece of plastic or rubber tubing over the junction where the hook joins the lure, as shown by the Brown-Godart spinner in Figure 13. These pieces of flexible tubing can be ob-

FIGURE 13.

SHOWING USE OF PLASTIC TUBING TO MAKE
LOOSE HOOK SEMIRIGID

tained from tackle stores and sometimes from drugstores. I like the colorless plastic variety best and usually carry a few inches of it in diameters between one-eighth and one-quarter inch.

HOW TO FISH SPINNERS

Unlike wobblers, spinners normally are fished in steadily, with little or no attempt at manipulating the lure. With many of them, one can feel in the rod grip the gentle throb of the swiftly revolving blade as it swings with the current or is being retrieved by the angler. Experience shows that there is an ideal speed for fishing every spinner; this being little more than enough to keep the blade turning steadily or to maintain proper level in the water. If the blade does not revolve readily, a slight twitch of the rod tip should make it do so. If not, it may be because the clevis which secures the blade has become bent or clogged. When this happens, the angler usually can remedy the trouble but, if he cannot, it may be necessary to rerig the lure.

Incidentally, most experienced spinning anglers are opposed to using a snap swivel when fishing with spinning blade lures. The snap swivel is neither necessary nor desirable, being just one more thing to complicate the terminal tackle unnecessarily. It should not be used in an attempt to remedy line twisting because it is insufficient for the purpose. A Clinch Knot (see page 80) joins lure to line admirably and is so strong and easy to tie that nothing else is necessary.

In summary, a basic spinner assortment might include a long, narrow-bladed spinner; a short, wide-bladed spinner and a spinner with pronounced erratic, fluttering action. One or more of the smaller ones should have a dull-colored blade and one or more should be of the deep running type. This calls for about six different spinners as a minimum and about a dozen at the most. If they are selected for their intended uses, a fairly comprehensive assortment should not require more, except for one or two of the Adapter type shortly to be described.

CHARACTERISTICS OF WOBBLERS

The first wobbler undoubtedly was evolved from the bowl of a teaspoon, with handle sawed off and with holes bored at both ends for the split ring and hook and for the snap swivel. Since that day the wobbler, or wobbling spoon, in all its sizes, colors and designs, has been of paramount importance to fishermen.

Unlike the spinner, the wobbler should be used with a snap swivel or split ring in order to intensify its action. Unlike the spinner, the wobbler may be fished at varying speeds; frequently, the more erratic the better. Like the spinner, the wobbler may be allowed to sink and swing with the current. It also may be allowed to flutter down into the depths, being retrieved with a jerky motion of the rod tip for a short distance and then being allowed to sink back again.

HOW TO FISH WOBBLERS

To learn to fish a wobbler correctly, it is helpful to practice where one can watch its action in the water. When free of the tension of the line, it sinks more erratically than a falling leaf on a windless day; so much so, in fact, that many fish take it as it is going down. Retrieved under the manipulation of the rod, the wobbler returns in an even more erratic manner. Some fish like it best when it is fished slowly. At other times, a faster and more lively action brings best results. Variation in these methods of fishing is a good rule until the fish indicate their preference. I have seen trout and bass pursue the lure almost to my feet without taking it. A good twitch or two brings added life to the lure and often serves to make up their minds, usually to their regret.

DIFFERENCES IN STRUCTURAL TYPES

Wobbling spoons roughly may be classified into three structural types. One is the small, thick and relatively heavy but lightly cupped variety, used for fishing deep in lakes or pools or to enable the lure to sink more swiftly in very fast currents. An excellent example is the Wob-L-Rite illustrated in "Typical Spinners and Wobblers." A second type, such as the Goldfish or Phoebe, is lighter, longer and thinner. This has the advantage of landing more delicately on the water and of holding in a normal current so that it will not sink too readily and become caught on the bottom where water is shallow. The third type is thin, long, wide and more heavily cupped for particularly erratic action, as illustrated by the Dardevle. It is maximumly useful in waters of medium depth. All of these lures cast uncommonly well, but, for longest casts, the first-mentioned type is superior because of its greater weight in proportion to its size. It will be noted that some wobblers are bent downward slightly at the head. This gives them a planing action in addition to the side-to-side wobble caused by the cup.

Many wobblers are furnished in natural metal; us-

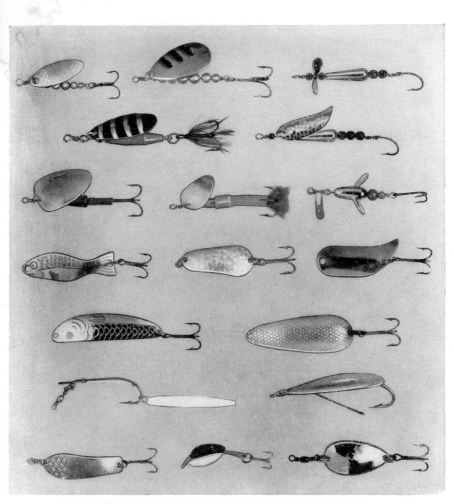

TYPICAL SPINNERS AND WOBBLERS

(L to R) *Rockland C. P. Swing, Rockland Flirt, Lyford Proptic,
Garcia Abu Reflex, Lyford Birdwing,
Garcia Virex, Airex Preska Perch, St. Claire Tail-Lite,
Stuart Goldfish, Seneca Wob-L-Rite, Lyford Birdwing,
Seneca Side-Winder, Eppinger Dardevle,
South Bend Trix Oreno, Johnson Silver Spoon,
Orvis Long Spoon, Hayden Multi-Wag, Garcia Safir*

TYPICAL PLUGS AND OTHER LURES SUITABLE FOR
FRESH WATER SPINNING

(L to R) *Barracuda Super Midget, Tulsa Bee, Heddon Tiny Runt,
Heddon Tiny Torpedo, South Bend Midg-Oreno, Phillips
Midget Killer,*
Tulsa Bizzy Bee, Phillips Weedless Popper,
Heddon Tiny Lucky 13, Helin Flatfish, Longendyke Moth,
*Garcia Pecos Eelet, Barracuda Baby Dude, Lily Bay
Moosehead Minny,*
*weighted streamer fly (cast body); weighted steelhead
fly (wire body); Pequea Quilby Minnow*

ually brass or copper. Their action and their relative brightness seem more important than their color. As with the spinners, some should be dull for bright days and some bright for dull ones, or for discolored water. If they want to corrode in the tackle box, I let them do so, and I carry a treated metal polishing cloth to rub them up to the desired brightness when advisable. It is easy to polish a dull blade when the occasion calls for it, but rather difficult quickly to dull down a bright one. My favorite polishing material is the "Blitz" cloth, with which every man who has been in the service is familiar. It blackens with use, but a piece six inches square will last for months. Added to these, a colored wobbler always is desirable, but owning more than one or two seems unnecessary. The red-and-white striped Dardevle is a perennial favorite in this category, particularly when the underside is of copper.

Nearly all of these wobbling spoons are connected to their hooks by means of a split ring, so it is easy to remove the customary treble hook and to substitute a single, or one of a different size, when desirable. With these lures, hooks dressed with hair or feathers often are more resultful than the bare hooks. Accordingly, I carry a few dressed hooks and use them when the occasion seems to warrant. In pond or lake fishing they are particularly productive. Red and white, blue and white, or yellow and white are good combinations and, to my mind, polar bear hair is better than anything else because it has a translucent glistening sheen which is very attractive to fish. If the reader cannot dress his own hooks, he most certainly can find a fly-tying friend who can do this for him until he collects the meager equipment and knowledge necessary to do it himself.

WEIGHTED FLIES
AND HOW TO WEIGHT THEM

I am not one of the relatively few who think that weighted flies are desirable in spinning. As a method, spinning is very comprehensive, but it should not be expected to be a cure-all for everything! Fly-fishing is best done with the fly rod although, in some cases, the plastic ball (to be described in the next chapter) makes artificial flies or nymphs amazingly productive when used with spinning tackle.

Good weighted wet flies for spinning can be purchased in most tackle shops and we can make them by winding the body of a long shanked hook with wire, as shown in Figure 14. We can crimp a large split shot at the head, or can mold the body with lead and put the dressing of a streamer fly or bucktail over it to make a weighted fly which can be cast reasonably well. The correct way to wind a wire-bodied fly is rather tedious, but is described in detail in my book *Streamer Fly Fishing in Fresh and Salt Water*. When all is said and done, I think the result, in fresh water fishing, is much less advantageous than using wobblers, spinners or plugs. Weighted flies are so logy in action

FIGURE 14.

EXAMPLES OF WEIGHTED FLIES FOR SPINNING

*Body at left is wound with copper wire; fly at right has
a painted lead bead-head.*

that they are almost useless in slack water. They are
fast water lures, if anything, and even in fast water I
have invariably found something else to be better.

HOW TO SELECT AND TO FISH PLUGS

Those of us who enjoy seeking certain species of
game fish, and particularly the largemouthed or smallmouthed bass, will find a few small plugs to be valuable additions to our collection of lures. Here again,
action seems more important than color, although I
am sure there are some who will not agree with such a
statement. In any event, it seems tactful to leave arguments about colors to others and to confine these remarks to the three important types of plugs and to
their intended uses.

I enjoy seeing a big bass erupt from the depths and
smash at a lure on the surface, and so I like using the
surface plug most of all. Some of the plugs of this type

are built with concave heads, and often have tails of hair or feathers. The concave head, as shown in the illustrations of "Typical Plugs," makes a popping splash when the rod tip is twitched. Usually, these plugs are cast to openings in the lily pads, to deep shore-line holes between rocks, or to some other spot where a big bass is likely to be. They should be allowed to rest there for part of a minute before being brought into action. When the rings caused by the cast have disappeared, the angler gives his rod a light twitch to move the plug ever so slightly. If nothing happens, a more pronounced twitch, or a series of them, will cause the little plug to pop and to splash on the surface with the hoped-for result that the bass will throw discretion to the winds and grab the lure with a resounding splash and a breath-taking leap. Plugs of the popping type, or of the crawling and similar varieties, are especially useful where there are obstructions under the surface. They also are favorite lures when the bass come into the shallows along about sundown to feed.

A second variety is the type of plug which floats on the surface when at rest but which dives and darts underwater when being retrieved. These usually have a cupped or a flat metal or plastic scoop just behind the eye of the lure to make them dive when the angler reels them in. The larger the scoop or lip, the deeper is the lure's tendency to dive. Such lures give best results when the speed of the retrieve is varied and when the rod tip is jerked occasionally. This gives them an intensely erratic motion and causes them to swim at varying depths underwater. Once in a while anglers find it rewarding to let them come to the surface before making them dive again, in order to create a surface commotion, which seems to be very alluring to bass.

The third type is the sinking plugs, which are most useful for exploring deep water. Some of them have small propellers at the front or at both front and rear to give them added action, or turbulence. They are allowed to sink close to the bottom and then are jerked and retrieved for a few feet, after which the same action is repeated.

The few examples of "Typical Plugs" shown in the full-page illustrations are not intended to indicate preference but merely to exemplify the variety of types. If we were to illustrate and describe all of the good plugs available, this book would be compelled to accomplish that and little more! Every section of the country has its favorites, and what is one man's meat may be another's poison. The spinning angler interested in plugging is well advised to select two or three locally popular examples of each type in the sizes and weights called for by the power of his tackle. This gives a range for all occasions — and it is safe to say that, if this modest collection does not produce results, it would be preferable to go in for dinner rather than to continue fishing.

USES OF ADAPTERS

Last, but not least, among artificial lures for spinning is the adapter, three of which are shown in Figure 15. This ordinarily is a spinner, and the weighted body necessary for casting it may be slid up,

FIGURE 15.

THREE TYPES OF ADAPTERS

to open the wire loop, so that any sort of ringed eye streamer fly or hook for bait may be attached for casting or for trolling. Other versions are equipped with a snap, as shown. One or two adapters are very handy because such a wide range of uses can be enjoyed with them.

REPAIRS AND RERIGGING

A few years ago I was fishing a stream at low water and saw numerous lures in various stages of disrepair which had been caught on the bottom when the water was higher. Perhaps because my grandmother was of Scottish ancestry, I felt compelled to pick them up and to bring them home. Then it occurred to me that I had kept a good many broken lures in the hope that someday I could get someone to fix them.

Shortly afterwards, an angler dropped in to talk fishing. Upon being shown this rather disreputable array of junk, he remarked, "Why don't you fix 'em yourself? It's easy! If you have some small round-nosed pliers and some stiff wire, I'll show you how."

He spent the rest of the evening instructing me in the various ways of making and repairing lures, and I have been an intent scavenger ever since. Gradually I collected a kit of tools, wire, beads, weighted bodies, clevises, blades, hooks, split rings and other parts, thus enabling me to make a wide variety of spinners and similar lures according to my own desires and at a considerable saving to the pocketbook.

To do this, it only is necessary to start with a few essentials, which most hardware stores or tackle shops can furnish. These include:

A pair of very small round-nosed pliers
A pair of small wire cutting nippers
A coil or two of stainless steel leader wire in sizes averaging about Number 9 or Number 10
A dozen or two clevises of various sizes
A dozen or two split rings of various sizes
A dozen or two assorted treble- and single-ringed eye hooks

We can collect all broken or unwanted lures and unstring them, discarding the wire and other unusable parts and retaining everything worth saving. Hooks, unless badly rusted, can be cleaned and resharpened. Spinner blades can be polished and can be lacquered by dipping them in thin fly dressing cement. Beads,

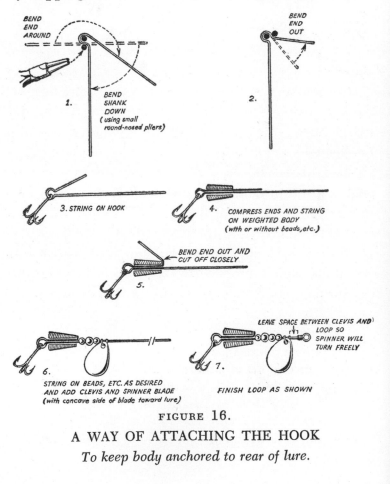

FIGURE 16.

A WAY OF ATTACHING THE HOOK

To keep body anchored to rear of lure.

weighted bodies and many other parts can be used again and again.

RIGGING LURES

Figures 16 to 18 describe several of the simple ways of rigging lures. These mainly concern making and re-

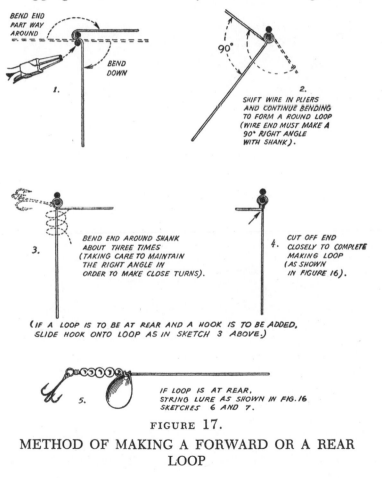

FIGURE 17.

METHOD OF MAKING A FORWARD OR A REAR LOOP

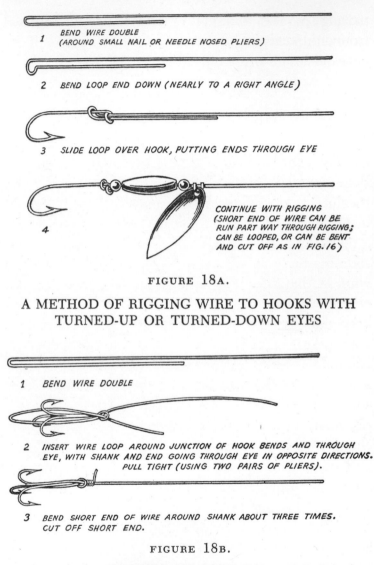

1 BEND WIRE DOUBLE
   (AROUND SMALL NAIL OR NEEDLE NOSED PLIERS)

2   BEND LOOP END DOWN (NEARLY TO A RIGHT ANGLE)

3   SLIDE LOOP OVER HOOK, PUTTING ENDS THROUGH EYE

4   CONTINUE WITH RIGGING
    (SHORT END OF WIRE CAN BE
    RUN PART WAY THROUGH RIGGING;
    CAN BE LOOPED, OR CAN BE BENT
    AND CUT OFF AS IN FIG. 16)

FIGURE 18A.

A METHOD OF RIGGING WIRE TO HOOKS WITH
TURNED-UP OR TURNED-DOWN EYES

1   BEND WIRE DOUBLE

2   INSERT WIRE LOOP AROUND JUNCTION OF HOOK BENDS AND THROUGH
    EYE, WITH SHANK AND END GOING THROUGH EYE IN OPPOSITE DIRECTIONS.
    PULL TIGHT (USING TWO PAIRS OF PLIERS).

3   BEND SHORT END OF WIRE AROUND SHANK ABOUT THREE TIMES.
    CUT OFF SHORT END.

FIGURE 18B.

ANOTHER METHOD OF RIGGING WIRE TO A
TREBLE HOOK

pairing spinners, although wobblers can be fashioned from cheap teaspoons or from flat pieces of brass if the necessary tools are handy. Blades and spoons can be coated with plastic paint or enamel in various colors.

MAKING AN ADAPTER

It may also be helpful to describe the method of making adapters, such as are shown in Figure 15. Begin by making a forward loop in the wire and string the lure from the front, leaving a sliding weighted metal body or a large bead of metal at the rear. Make a rear loop as shown in Figure 16, Sketches 1–4, and slide the body forward, cutting off enough of the end wire so that the body will slide back over it, thus closing the loop securely. The spring of the wire will keep the body from sliding forward until the fisherman desires to change the hook. Another type of adapter is shown in Figure 19. Make the rear snap shown in Sketches 1–3; dress the wire as desired, and add the forward loop as has been described. With this rig, many types of hooks and flies can be added, or changed as seems advisable.

If one wishes to make or repair his own spinning lures, this provides the opportunity of trying out individual ideas and of adapting lures to a wide variety of purposes. If, for example, a hook is too small or too large, it is a matter of but a few minutes to cut it off and to restring the lure with a more suitable one. If a clevis becomes broken, the lure can be repaired, or

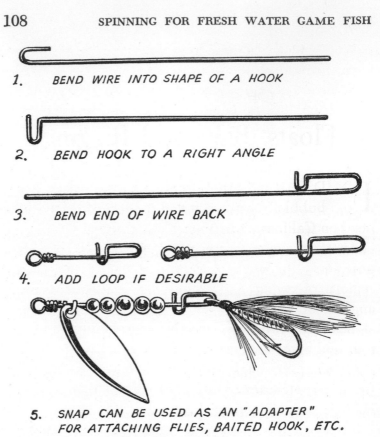

1.   *BEND WIRE INTO SHAPE OF A HOOK*

2.   *BEND HOOK TO A RIGHT ANGLE*

3.   *BEND END OF WIRE BACK*

4.   *ADD LOOP IF DESIRABLE*

5.   *SNAP CAN BE USED AS AN "ADAPTER"
     FOR ATTACHING FLIES, BAITED HOOK, ETC.*

FIGURE 19.

A METHOD OF MAKING A SNAP

Use round-nosed pliers to make bends as small as possible. If bends are not creased, thus weakening the wire, this snap will be strong and serviceable.

if a bit more or less weight should be included, this easily can be done. My kit goes with me wherever I can take it on fishing trips and it has saved the day more than once when I am far away from tackle stores.

CHAPTER FIVE

Floats, Baits and Rigging

I PAID FAR too little attention to the plastic float, or "bubble," until we found it successful for steelhead on California's famous Klamath River.

Another angler and I were trying our spinning gear along the productive riffles in the Happy Camp region, preceded and followed by several fly rod anglers. Almost everyone was taking an occasional fish — beautiful fresh-run steelhead, weighing between four and eight pounds.

My companion rummaged through his kit, searching for a "secret weapon" among his collection of lures. He held up a little plastic ball float.

"Ever try the plastic float with a wet fly?" he inquired.

I remember saying that I preferred using the fly rod for fly-fishing and that I thought spinning tackle worked best with weighted lures.

Of course that is true to a large extent, but the fact was impressed upon me, on that day, that the plastic float can offer wonderfully productive results with flies in spinning. It is equally valuable for handling many varieties of baits, which can be fished in novel and very resultful ways. It has the advantage of being an adjustable casting weight as well as a float which, by partly filling it with water, can be given any de-

15/16″ DIA.   *1 3/16″ DIA.*

FIGURE 20.

PLASTIC BALL FLOATS

Cap is removed to fill float with water to give desired weight for casting. In this one, called the "Buldo," the cap is anchored to the inside of the float to prevent losing it.

sired degree of buoyancy. When fully filled, it sinks slowly and is superior to lead weights for many purposes. (Figure 20.)

The angler rigged his float as shown in Figure 21, using an ordinary wet steelhead fly on the dropper, and filling the float full of water to make it sink. He cast the rig to the opposite bank of the river, allowing the current to swing the float in a wide arc, with the little fly trailing along behind. Just as the bubble completed its swing he felt a heavy strike; played the fish and led it to the beach. He took four steelhead in rapid succession while no other angler in sight had

taken more than one. As an experiment, we swapped
tackle. He fished ahead of me, using a wobbler that
was the favorite on the river at that time. With the
float and fly rig, I took three fish to his one. In our

FIGURE 21.

A METHOD OF RIGGING THE PLASTIC FLOAT
FOR USE WITH WET FLIES

group of four anglers, the fly and bubble combination
accounted for more steelhead than the other three
rods combined, and the two fly-fishermen who were
with us had been using the same pattern of fly!

USES OF THE PLASTIC BALL FLOAT

Since then, I have seen the plastic ball float produce equally well many times. Anglers who don't use

it are missing a large part of the fun and of the results of spinning. It can be employed in numerous ways. Some anglers attach the float to the end of the line and then add about two feet of leader, with the fly fastened to the end of the rig. This works fairly well with bait, but not particularly so with flies because, with the ball between fly and angler, the angler has more difficulty in feeling the strike and in setting the hook unless the buoyancy of the rig is adjusted with great care.

The preferable method of rigging for wet flies consists of tying about four feet of monofilament to the monofilament line with a Barrel Knot so that about two or three feet of this acts as a tippet to which the ball is fastened and a lesser amount as a dropper to which the fly is attached. A second dropper can be added if desired, with the bubble and the knots for the droppers spaced about two feet apart. When any air is left in the bubble we have noted that it will float. When completely filled, it will sink. Having approximately the same specific gravity as the water around it, the filled ball will not sink quickly and catch bottom (as lead might) but rather will drift as deep in the current as the angler allows. Aided by the lightness of the line, it has a tendency to remain in the fast current and thus it can work a fly down a run or riffle even on the far side of the stream. The bubble casts beautifully, making it easy to fish the fly at a distance of over a hundred feet, even from in front of or from under foliage. This length of cast is an accomplishment

Jim Deren, of New York's famed "Angler's Roost,"
Shows a Pretty Angler How to Go Spinning for Bass

"Talking Tackle" Is One of the Pleasures of Spinning

rather difficult for many fly rod anglers, and one which is impossible under adverse conditions.

The several brands of plastic ball floats available differ in quality more widely than one might suppose. Colorless plastic is superior to the colored type because it is more nearly invisible in the water. The cheaper floats are unpolished and their rough edges have a tendency to cut the line. The Buldo illustrated (Figure 20) is a French import and I think it is the original of its type. It may cost slightly more than some others, but it is smooth and beautifully made, with a fine monofilament fastener to keep the little cap from dropping off. This is an important improvement because the caps otherwise are easy to lose and they sometimes fly off in casting. All such floats have two holes on opposite sides of the rim for attaching line or leader. I like a Clinch Knot for this purpose because it is strong and minimumly visible. A large Perfection Loop Knot, with the loop threaded through the hole and put around the float, works fairly well. Although anglers have told me that they have known of instances where a fish has struck at the float, rather than at the lure, I never have seen this happen. The float looks so much like a bubble in the water that fish normally ignore it, and never are frightened by it unless it is handled carelessly on a smooth surface.

A favorite and very productive method of using the plastic float is as shown in Figure 22. The float is fastened three or four feet forward of a short dropper on which a dry fly is tied. The fly should be a good floater and should be oiled to keep it on the surface. The bubble is cast crossstream, or crossstream and down, and is allowed to float with the current on a fairly tight line. To do this, the angler probably will elect to leave the pickup arm of his reel open and to control the line by paying it out gradually, regulated by the pressure of his forefinger on the front face of the spool. The rod is held high to keep the dry fly above water. In this position, the angler can twitch his rod tip to make the fly dance and skitter about just over the surface and on it, much as a natural fly acts when laying eggs. The motion of the fly seems to excite fish greatly and they usually will rush in from long distances to jump at it. When water is clear in a woodland pool it is a great thrill to see trout race for the dancing fly and splash for it on the surface.

The ball float also is excellent for nymph fishing. It can be rigged as in B in Figure 22 so the nymph can drift a foot or more below the surface. Fish often take nymphs so delicately that they may spit them out before the angler knows they are there. But the plastic ball usually signals even the lightest strike by a pause in its travel or by unusualness in its bobbing on the surface. If the angler watches it, he usually can tell when a fish has taken the lure. A light strike (if the hook is as sharp as it should be) should hook the fish and will not move the ball from its position to any extent, allowing it to continue its travel if the fish

does not become hooked. The methods of dapping the
fly and of using the subsurface drifting nymph may be
used on the same rig (as the illustration shows); oftentimes with great success.

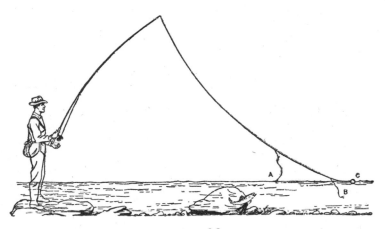

FIGURE 22.

A METHOD OF "DAPPING" WITH WET OR DRY
FLY AND THE PLASTIC BALL

*A is the fly. B is a nymph added optionally to drift below
surface. C is the plastic ball.*

Another method of fishing the deeply drifting
nymph is shown in Figure 23. Here, the partly filled
ball connects the line and two or three feet of leader,
to which is fastened an artificial nymph (or a baited
hook). A split shot or two can be added to the leader
to keep the lure well below the surface. This rig will
keep the nymph in a current even when fishing far
across the stream. The length of the leader can be ad-

justed to the stream's depth so that the lure will drift a foot or two from the bottom. The rig also works well in pond fishing, where the bait must be kept just above weed beds. In such a situation, it is an ideal hookup for using live shiners.

FIGURE 23.

SURFACE DRIFTING RIG FOR NYMPHS OR
SMALL BAITS

The point originally was made that when the ball is attached behind the lure it is more difficult to hook fish than when it is rigged as shown in Figure 21. This difficulty can be overcome in a very simple way. It is important to adjust the weight so that the ball barely will float. This calls for careful balance between the amount of water in the ball and the weight of the lure and split shot used below it. When the ball barely floats, the fish feel almost no drag on the lure and thus are less inclined to spit it out. Anglers who have trouble hooking fish should find that proper adjustment of the tackle will solve the problem.

An alternate method of getting a bait down into currents (very popular in steelhead fishing) calls for putting a small barrel swivel between leader and line, as shown in Figure 24. String the float on the leader

FIGURE 24.

DEEP DRIFTING RIG FOR WET FLIES, EGG CLUSTERS OR OTHER BAIT

through one eye of the float only, so that it will run freely between bait and swivel. When the bait is cast, the float will be next to the hook, but when it lands, the bait will drop and the ball will slip up the leader until it is stopped by the swivel. Thus, the bait (worms or fish eggs, usually) will be drifting along in the flow of the current, as close to the bottom as the length of the leader allows.

Many situations in bait fishing call for keeping the bait just off the bottom of a pool or pond or slowly moving stream. Figure 25 shows a way to do this. A

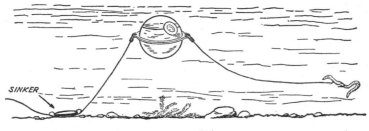

FIGURE 25.

SINKER AND FLOAT METHOD OF HOLDING BAIT OFF BOTTOM

small lead is pinched to the line two or three feet behind the bubble, which may be partly filled with
water. Both lead and bubble aid the weight necessary
for casting. The baited hook is connected to the bubble
by a piece of monofilament, which also is about two
feet long. The lead holds the bottom and the bubble
seeks to rise to the surface, thus keeping the bait
where it belongs. Before casting this rig, it is well to
try it in shallow water in a similar current to that in
which it will be used. The lead must be heavy enough
to hold and the bubble must have enough buoyancy
to keep the lure off the bottom (but not much more
so, in order to put minimum drag on the lure).

These are some of the ways of rigging the plastic
ball float; there are many more, just as fascinating and
productive for the bait fisherman as for those who prefer artificial lures. The methods mentioned should illustrate that the plastic ball, as used with spinning
tackle, offers advantages found nowhere else in angling; advantages that aid good luck in fishing and that
add to the fun of catching fish.

USES OF KEELS; HOW TO MAKE THEM

In the earlier days of American spinning, the twisting of lines, caused largely by improperly made lures,
was considered a necessary evil. Line twisting still is
an evil, but fortunately it now is entirely unnecessary.
We have noted that swivels offer inadequate advantages in preventing line twist. A keel of the proper

size, made either from plastic, lead or from some other metal, should prevent line twist entirely. This is especially important in trolling, where line twist usually causes spinning fishermen a great deal of trouble. A few keels of various sizes and weights, both of plastic and of lead, are necessities in almost any spinning kit. I find myself using them less and less, largely because I have learned to shun lures that twist lines, but they still are valuable on occasion.

In near-surface trolling, and in top-water casting with lures that are known or presumed to be twisters,

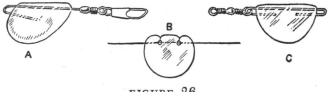

FIGURE 26.

TYPICAL PLASTIC KEELS

a plastic keel will meet requirements, unless the added weight of one of lead is needed. Figure 26 illustrates three typical keels. A is of colorless molded plastic, produced by Herschel, of New York City. B is stamped from a plastic sheet and is so made that the line can be slipped through the two slots into holes as shown. C is made by bending and cementing plastic sheeting around wire. Plastic keels can be cut or punched from colorless plastic, but they are more secure, especially in larger sizes, when cemented around a looped wire.

When cut to size, they can be bent double by heating the plastic at the bend with the dull edge of a moderately hot kitchen knife blade. Then double the plastic around the wire by pressing the flat of a blade against it. The two sides can be bonded together, thus holding the plastic securely to the wire, by cementing the crevice with plastic fly-dressing lacquer. Looping the wire is a very simple matter. Knowing how to make keels allows fishermen to suit their individual tastes, but there are so many inexpensive types on the market that usually it is more logical to buy them than to bother with making them.

Lead keels prevent the twisting of lines, aid in manipulating lures at lower levels in the water, and

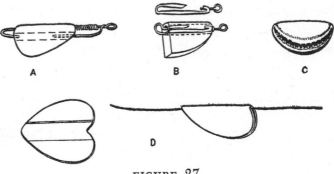

FIGURE 27.

TYPICAL LEAD KEELS

supplement the weight of the lure to provide longer casts. Some rather elaborate ones, such as are shown in sketches A and B in Figure 27, are made in this country and also are being imported from abroad. The body of the Schnell keel (shown in A) slides forward against a spring, to allow hooking on lure or line. The French keel (shown in B) comes in several sizes, the body sliding over the forward loop to expose a hook on which a lure or line can be attached. C is a much simpler "clamshell" variety; merely a foldover of lead which is heavier in the lower part and which is scored on the inside of the fold to grip the line securely. A favorite of mine is the easily obtainable Pflueger heart-shaped lead keel (shown in D). This can be purchased in several sizes and works very well both as a keel and as a casting weight. Those who make their own lures frequently use this type of lead to weight the heads, painting it with enamel in various colors and designs.

Small-diameter tubing or flat strips of lead or other soft metals usually can be found readily and can be

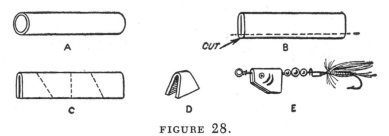

FIGURE 28.

A METHOD OF MAKING LEAD KEELS

A—Lead Tubing. B—Flatten and Cut. C—Cut into Sections. D—Open for Crimping on Line or Wire. E—Paint for Use on Lures.

cut easily into keels as shown in the sketches in Figure 28. As illustrated in sketch E, these leads can be used for weighting many varieties of spinning lures, as well as for keeling and weighting lines.

When the steadying effect of a keel is not needed, ordinary sinkers and split shot of various sizes are very adaptable for weighting spinning lures and lines to extend the distance of the cast or to permit fishing at greater depths. A split shot can be crimped just back of the eye over the shank of a long hook and can be enameled and decorated to represent the eye of a fish. Then the fly can be dressed as desired. These obviously are lightweight lures, but are extremely valuable in fishing for small pond and stream fish where long casts are unnecessary. Small propellers (obtainable from fly-tying material suppliers) can be strung on lures of this type when the hooks are wired as previously described. These small propellers add just enough flash and action to be enticing as an embellishment. I have found this sort of lure to be one of the best for crappies and, on occasion, for trout in small streams.

"PENCIL TYPE" LEADS FOR DEEP DRIFTING

One of the greatest drawbacks to deep fishing is the annoying propensity of leads to become caught up between rocks and other obstructions on the bottom, often at the expense of losing the entire terminal rigging and sometimes part of the line as well. This trouble is especially prevalent on the salmon and steel-head rivers of the Northwest, where winter fish lie deep in holding positions in turbulent waters and re-fuse to move very far for either bait or fly. One must drift the lure naturally and very near to the bottom, bringing it close to the fish in order to induce a strike.

Since ordinary leads become too frequently caught up by such fishing, anglers in northern California, Oregon and Washington developed the "pencil type" of lead shown in Figure 29. Originally these were used only in casting and trolling with heavy tackle,

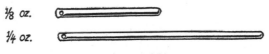

$\frac{1}{8}$ oz.

$\frac{1}{4}$ oz.

FIGURE 29.

"PENCIL TYPE" DRIFT LEADS

and therefore were of larger sizes than shown, usually being a quarter of an inch in diameter and weighing from one to four ounces.

When spinning became popular, smaller and lighter leads were needed, and are being made in one-eighth-inch diameters to weigh one eighth, one quarter and one half of an ounce (by the Cummings Machine Works, of Salem, Oregon, and others). They are at-tached to the rigging by two- or three-pound-test monofilament, tied to a cross-line swivel as shown in Figure 30. Their pencil shape usually prevents them from becoming caught between rocks on the stream bed and, when they do become caught, they are inclined to bend and to pull loose. The worst that can happen is to break the light connection of monofilament, thus losing the lead but saving the rest of the tackle.

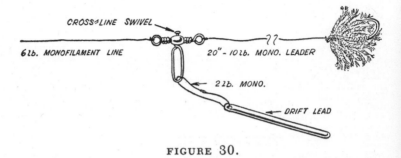

CROSS-LINE SWIVEL

6 lb. MONOFILAMENT LINE

20" - 10 lb. MONO. LEADER

2 lb. MONO.

DRIFT LEAD

FIGURE 30.

WESTERN-TYPE DRIFT RIG FOR STEELHEAD
AND SALMON

This hookup is very popular for fishing with salmon eggs on Western rivers and, to a similar extent, with certain types of flies. One of these, which may be taken by the fish for a salmon-egg cluster, is the Red Rag shown in the above illustration. This is tied entirely from Radiant Red nylon yarn wound around the short hook and also tied in at the head in a bunch of many ends (cut off as long as the hook) in a manner which makes the lure resemble a short, wide tassel. Reports from famous Western anglers, such as Don Harger of Salem, Oregon, indicate that the Red Rag frequently is even more successful than the ever-popular egg clusters. In this rig it will be noted that the leader is considerably stronger than the line as a protection against the teeth of big buck chinooks, silver salmon and steelhead. The pencil lead (as long as six-and-a-half inches in the one-half-ounce weight) is so rigged that the over-all length from lead and to swivel is about eight inches. This allows the lead to guide the lure close to the bottom, over rocks and other obstructions.

When this rig is used, the cast is made in the run or drift across- and upstream. The line is allowed to remain slack for only as long as it takes for the lead to reach bottom. Then the slack is taken up and the rod is held high so that the main current of the river will not catch the line and pull the lure out of the pockets and eddies the angler desires to fish. As the line swings toward the fisherman, he lets out more gradually (with the pickup arm of the reel open) to enable the lead to "walk" along the river bottom with the current. Each bump easily can be felt in the rod. The fish usually takes the lure so delicately that it is difficult to feel the strike. Therefore, when the lure seems to stop, and no bumping of the lead is felt, it is a signal to strike — and to strike *hard*. The fish, in jumping, usually snaps off the lead, enabling the angler to play him, without this weight, on the lightest and sportiest gear.

I have gone into some detail to describe this method because it is one of the most intelligent solutions so far advanced for fishing rivers close to the bottom without the annoyance of getting caught up frequently. Quite obviously, the rig is as good for deep trolling as it is for casting.

METHODS OF RIGGING MINNOWS AND OTHER BAITS

Since new and improved artificial lures have become so abundant and so available, the formerly popular habit of spinning with minnow rigs has fallen into a decline. Minnows often are rather difficult to obtain and always are a nuisance to keep fresh and to hook up properly. I must confess to being rather biased in disfavor of them, largely because I have reached the conclusion that many artificial lures are fully as productive and are a lot easier to use. Minnow fishing, however, has its advocates and, undoubtedly, its advantages. The confirmed minnow-fisherman usually is so expert at his art and is so partial to one form of rigging or another that I hesitate to add my suggestions to this book. I only do so with the thought that beginners may find them of value.

The English have used baitfish in their more comprehensive versions of spinning for as long as the method has existed. So have the French — and others. They have developed diabolical multi-hooked contrivances such as the Crocodile Spinner, and others equally awesome which I refuse to mention. Only one of them has taken root in America and, in its least pretentious arrangement of hooks, it looks like the sketch in Figure 31. As this sketch shows, a nail-like prong is pushed into the minnow's gullet and the hooks are embedded in his sides and near the tail to give the minnow a slight wobble or spin in the water.

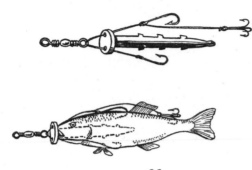

FIGURE 31.

A WEIGHTED MINNOW GANG AND A METHOD
OF RIGGING MINNOWS FOR CASTING

About the only credit I can give this rig is to say that it is a notorious line-twister and undoubtedly is one of the things "purists" refer to when they say that they disapprove of spinning.

There are, however, two other methods of rigging minnows for spinning which are fully as easy, and much more innocuous. Figure 32 shows a method of rigging a minnow with a single hook, which should be so inserted that it will curve the body slightly, thus giving it a wobbling motion or an extremely slow spin. If it is curved insufficiently, it cannot be fished naturally enough to be much of a temptation to the fish.

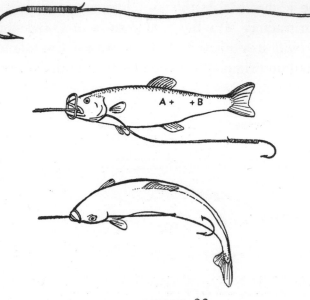

FIGURE 32.

METHOD OF RIGGING UNWEIGHTED MINNOWS

Use snelled minnow hook. Work hook through mouth and out of the gills, making a half-hitch around jaws with leader to keep mouth closed. Insert hook at "A" and out at "B" so that shank of hook is completely imbedded. Adjust leader so that minnow will be curved slightly.

If curved too much, it will spin rapidly and cause the line to become badly twisted. It will, however, cast so well that added weight normally is unnecessary except to sink it deeply. To keep such a bait from twisting the line, a small keel lead followed by a swivel or two can be rigged a foot or more back from the lure.

If one wishes to fish minnows, live ones usually are more satisfactory. The best way I know of to rig them so they will stay on the hook for several casts is as illustrated in Figure 33. The needle should be run through the minnow lengthwise just above the back-

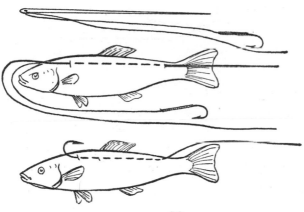

FIGURE 33.

A METHOD OF HOOKING A LIVE MINNOW
FOR CASTING

*Using a surgical needle to thread monofilament length-
wise above backbone.*

bone so that it will not pierce the organs. When the hook is properly in place, the length of monofilament used for threading can be tied to the line by a Barrel Knot. Usually, a small split shot or two should be added to the line, particularly if one wishes the bait to sink in a current.

If one does not wish to go to this bother, the minnow can be hooked in the fleshy part of the body by passing the hook once through the back, just below and behind the dorsal fin (taking care not to hit the backbone). The minnow may not stay on the hook as well when attached by this means, but this method is used in still-fishing, where only one cast usually is necessary.

The backbone should not be touched, since this will kill the minnow. Dead minnows should be rigged so that they can be fished head forward in order to give them lifelike swimming action. The hook is fastened near the rear because game fish strike at a fast-moving bait at the rear or at the middle of the body. On the other hand, as shown in Figure 33, a live minnow normally is taken head-first, and the hook is placed near the head for this reason.

PORK RINDS AND STRIP BAITS

One of the greatest joys in spinning, as far as bait fishermen are concerned, falls to the man who enjoys using worms and never before has tried to cast them with spinning gear. A hook baited with an average-sized worm will travel to an almost unbelievable distance if a light enough line is used, even without the aid of split shot. An equal thrill comes to the bass fisherman when he casts out a small pork chunk and skitters it near the grasses or lily pads where feeding fish are so inclined to be. Many fishermen fasten a small, slender V-shaped piece of pork rind to the hook of a wobbler when fishing gets a bit dull. Often this produces results, but a similarly shaped piece cut from a white kid or chamois glove works fully as well and can be used again and again. One day my daughter's red balloon popped and some strips cut from that did wonderfully, too! In fact, wedge-shaped strips cut from rubber balloons are so fluttery and flexible that they are excellent attracters on almost any sort of lure. If we have learned the simple methods of winding wire into spinning lures (as described at the end of Chapter Four) it is easy to make the strip bait-hooking device shown in Figure 34 and to imagine many more uses to which it can be adapted. The combination shown, of a spinning blade and a wobbling blade, often works wonders, and I am surprised that it has not been used more extensively.

One could go on and on in describing the multitude of ways in which baits of every description can be used with spinning tackle, but space limitations make this impossible, and the many good books on bait fishing make it unnecessary. If crickets, grasshoppers, hellgrammites and similar favorite fish foods cannot be cast far enough, with or without the aid of a split shot or two, the little plastic ball nearly always can come to the rescue and permit far longer casts than usually are necessary. Wet flies, dry flies, nymphs, wobblers, spinners, plugs, bait and every other lure conceivable can be employed with such great advantage in spinning that this tackle seems to be the most comprehensive of any so far developed.

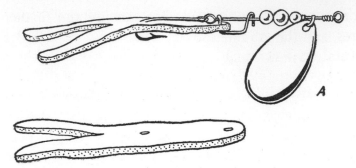

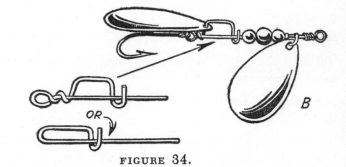

FIGURE 34.

HOOKING ARRANGEMENT FOR STRIP BAITS

The "Safety Pin" snap can be used for attaching pork rind, fishskin strips or similar baits, as shown in A; wobbler blades, as in B; with or without bucktail dressing on the hook.

WEEDLESS HOOKS

Now that we know how to bend stainless steel leader wire into spinning lures, it is a simple matter to fashion wire weed guards if we wish to do so. Fine wire of about size Number 2 is necessary for the smaller lures, and the examples in any plug box will show the several ways in which this can be done.

BUMPER LINES AND LEADERS

In spinning it would be difficult to find an instance where a leader should be used which is weaker than the line itself. If the tackle will hold with a light leader, we may as well use a line of similar strength because we can cast farther with a lighter line than with a heavier one. When lines and leaders are of the same strength and one gets hung up and must break loose, the break usually occurs at the leader knot or at the lure knot, thus saving the line — unless there is a weak spot in it.

While the leader should never be lighter than the line, there are many occasions when it should be heavier. An abnormally strong leader guards against the tackle being severed by the teeth of many varieties of fish. It enables us to land a large fish more easily when casting or trolling from a boat with a high deck or coaming. It enables us to cast heavier lures with lighter lines. In this latter category, the stronger and longer leader is called a "bumper line" and it usually extends from the lure to several turns around the reel spool. Its purpose is to prevent a heavy lure from being snapped off in casting when a very light line is being used. Many anglers complain of this, and fortunately the trouble can be dispelled by the use of a bumper line, which can be fastened to the casting line with a Barrel Knot. Usually, a bumper line is about half again as strong as the line itself, but this can be varied as circumstances dictate.

Except for purposes noted, leaders are unnecessary when monofilament lines are used, because the line itself is a leader. Braided lines should be attached to monofilament leaders about as long as the rod and of the same strength, or slightly stronger, than the line itself. The Barrel Knot joins the two nicely and slips easily through the guides.

HOW TO MAKE LEADERS

Metal leaders sometimes are necessary for use with sharp-teethed fish. Most of the metal leaders on sale in tackle stores are made for plug casting and are too heavy for spinning. The swivels with which they are equipped usually also are too large. Growing numbers of anglers are making up their own, providing any size and type of rigging for which the situation calls. Among the several excellent leader materials for this purpose are twisted bronzed stainless wire (such as is made by the Sevenstrand Tackle Manufacturing Company, of Long Beach, California) and nylon coated wire (called "Steelon," and made by the Berkley Fly Company, of Spirit Lake, Iowa). The former is available in 18-, 27- and 40-pound tests, and the latter in 20-, 30- and 45-pound tests. Both are amazingly fine, strong and flexible. The nylon coated wire seems less noticeable in the water than the uncoated varieties.

CRIMPING AND ALL-PURPOSE TOOLS

Tying leader loops in some of these materials is rather difficult. The Sevenstrand Company is one of those which furnishes a crimping tool and supplies of tiny tubular metal leader sleeves in appropriate sizes for the diameter of wire being used. These little sleeves easily can be crimped around loops of wire, to form strong and fine leaders which are very suitable for use in spinning.

This Sevenstrand crimping tool is rather heavy and bulky, and is confined to its one use. Many anglers prefer Sargent & Company's "Sportmate" tool (obtainable in sporting goods stores), which has crimping grooves built into its strong parallel action jaws. In recent seasons I never have gone fishing without a "Sportmate" (Figure 35) in my pocket because, in addition to its value for crimping leader sleeves and split shot, it is an excellent wire cutter and disgorger, plus being a serviceable pair of pliers as well. It can be used as a small wrench for fixing reels and for pulling or seating ferrules, and I even have found it handy as a streamside fly-tying vise. As the maker says, it is "A POCKET WORKSHOP IN ONE HANDY TOOL."

Finally, one of the most unnecessary of tragedies is to hook the proverbial "big one," play him carefully,

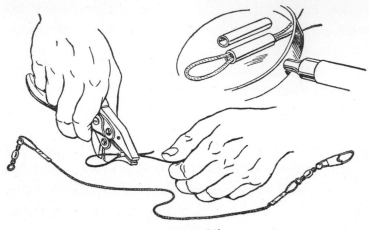

FIGURE 35.

"SPORTMATE" CRIMPING TOOL FOR LOOPING
FINE WIRE LEADERS

*In looping nylon coated wire, the nylon should be stripped
off the loop for added strength. The "Sportmate" tool also
is an excellent split shot crimper—and a handy disgorger,
pliers, wrench, hook and wire cutter, and a streamside fly
tying vise as well.*

maneuver him away from stumps and rocks, and bring
him safely toward the net — only to have him break
off, during a last flurry of activity, because the end of
the line has become weakened!

One should not have to lose a good fish or two in
this manner to learn the importance of breaking off
a foot or two of the terminal end occasionally. This
final few feet is the part of the line which absorbs
most of the shock and wear of casting, and, if not
eliminated from time to time, will become gradually

weaker and weaker. If the angler will remember to test it periodically and to break it off when necessary, this precaution will prevent the snapping off of many lures and the loss of important fish. When such cutting-back eventually removes too much, the line can be spliced with a partial spool of the same material (which should be saved for the purpose). If the splicing knot bothers the angler, the line can be reversed by winding it on to an extra reel spool.

CHAPTER SIX

On Choosing Spinning Rods

SPINNING ANGLERS frequently ask, "Which is more important; the rod, the reel, the lines or the lures?" Since any of these elements can contribute equally to landing or to losing fish, all are equally important. But errors in buying lines or lures can be corrected easily and economically, whereas poor judgment in selecting rods or reels is much more expensive.

While nearly any spinning rod, or so-called spinning rod, will do its work with a greater or lesser degree of perfection, the angler who knows enough to buy a really good one will find it to be a vital aid in fishing — and in the long run no more costly than one which does not operate nearly as well.

I must admit to being somewhat of an iconoclast about spinning rods. While many are excellent, it seems that others leave great room for improvement. It appears that a few manufacturers have produced them without bothering very much to find out exactly what an efficient spinning rod should be like. This state of affairs undoubtedly will continue until anglers learn to select the good ones and to spurn the rest.

To make matters worse, a few writers about spinning have given advice which seems highly improper.

They have set arbitrary lengths for rods without considering their power or purpose. They have advised buying rods by weight, when weight is highly misleading. They have made other pronouncements which seem to be ill-advised. Perhaps a lot of this is a matter of opinion, but experience proves that there are established facts which can be a fairly decisive guide to opinion. In this chapter I should like to outline several details about spinning rods which are the result of considerable experience. In the following chapter I should like to offer a new (and what seems to be a very sensible) guide to rod selection and to matching line strengths and lure weights, to make the tackle operate with maximum efficiency. I have no doubt that an hour or so devoted to absorbing this information will help fishermen to select equipment which will make casting easier and catching fish a lot more fun.

For the moment, we can ignore the materials from which spinning rods are made and concentrate on selecting a rod which has suitable action, whether it be of split bamboo, glass fiber, or something else.

ROD ACTION

A remark is frequently made that the action of a spinning rod should approximate a parabolic curve — or, in other words, that the rod should have "parabolic action." Figure 36 shows a typical parabolic curve. The simile is an apt one if it impresses upon our minds that a spinning rod gives maximum relative

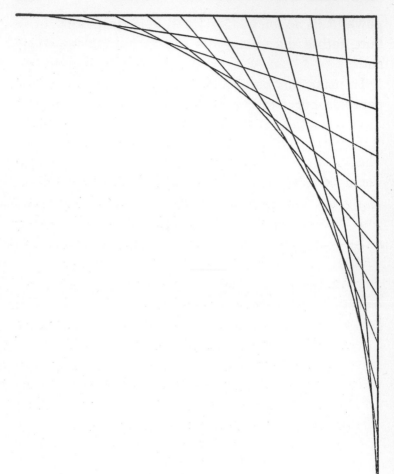

FIGURE 36.

A PARABOLIC CURVE

Under stress, the flexing of a spinning rod closely approximates a parabola.

power if its action is distributed uniformly from tip to butt, rather than being too soft or too stiff at either end.

To make this point more helpful, let's transfer this parabolic curve to Figure 37, where it is in the form of

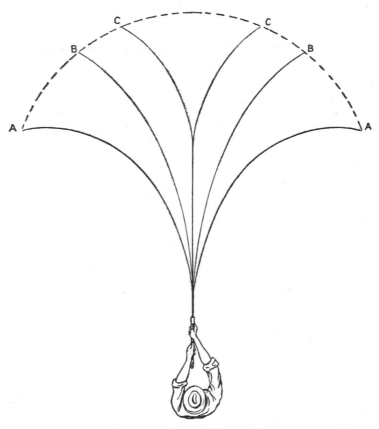

FIGURE 37.

PROPER AND IMPROPER FLEXING OF A
SPINNING ROD

a spinning rod being flexed to determine its action and an approximation of its power. To do this, grip the rod with both hands as shown and, with the butt held rigidly, cause it to flex from side to side as the illustration shows. Do this slowly at first, and then a bit faster, to gauge the curvature under varying degrees of stress.

While the rod is being oscillated, the flexing should be felt down into the grip itself. The action should be evenly distributed. Under moderate stress it should take the form of B-B, which usually is considered to be good medium action with ideal power. If it flexes easily to A-A it may be too soft in action, although this curve shows proper uniformity. If it flexes similar to C-C, the rod is too stiff in the butt and too light in the tip. This provides insufficient action and bears no relationship to the even distribution of power shown by the parabolic curve.

Thus, there are two things to be determined by this simple test. The flexing of the rod should be felt way down into the grip, and the rod should have gradually increasing curvature under stress.

Whether it is too soft or not can be decided in another way which is equally simple. In this test, make a false cast and bring the rod quickly to rest. The quivering of the tip should stop almost immediately. If the quivering does not damp down fast enough, the tip of the rod is too soft for proper power and accuracy in casting. This "tip quiver" works against the smooth outflow of the line, thereby penalizing the angler on distance and on precision in casting his lure.

These two tests need take only a minute for each rod examined, so it is easy to apply them to several rods and to pick out the better ones by process of elimination. The tests of course bear little or no relationship to the *quality* of the rod, which must be decided by other means shortly to be explained.

If one reflects upon these points for a few minutes, it will become clear that the distribution of power in a spinning rod is quite different from that of a fly rod or a plug casting rod. In order to get this so-called "parabolic" distribution of power down into the butt, the butt section must not be too stiff, but must be stiff enough to give the rod the action we have tried to describe. In order to reduce tip wobble or quivering to a minimum, the tip section must not be too soft.

Furthermore, let's note that, in arriving at this action, the length of the rod has been decided for us. There is an ideal length for the degree of power of every rod. If we increase or decrease the length of the butt and still retain proper spinning rod-action, the power of the rod will be increased or decreased accordingly. If we increase the length of the tip, this will serve only to soften the action of the rod and to increase its tendency for tip quiver and poor casting. Decreasing the length of the tip will add stiffness at the expense of ideal action.

Let's remember that when we say that the length of

the rod is thus established, we are discussing *ideal* action. It may be desirable to sacrifice this action to a degree in order to have a rod of certain power which is longer or shorter than normal for one reason or another. For example, we may want a shorter rod for fishing brushy streams where a longer one would interfere with casting. In this case, we can shorten the tip, thus harming the rod's action somewhat. Or we can shorten the butt, thus decreasing power and harming action correspondingly. We may want a longer rod to help us to cast over obstructions, such as in surf fishing. This must be obtained by lengthening the butt, since we would get too much tip wobble by lengthening the tip. In doing this, we still would impair the action of the rod, although perhaps with the compensation of the greater length.

From this, we can see that it would be difficult to get an ideal spinning rod by cutting down a fly rod or by adapting a plug casting stick to spinning. Yet I know of several well-known manufacturers who are doing this very thing. They sell these rods because the average spinning angler cannot distinguish between ideal action and action which is much less so. As anglers become better acquainted with tackle for spinning, it is logical to assume that such rods will be less prevalent.

Now, let's examine other aspects of spinning rods, particularly the grip, the ferrules and the guides.

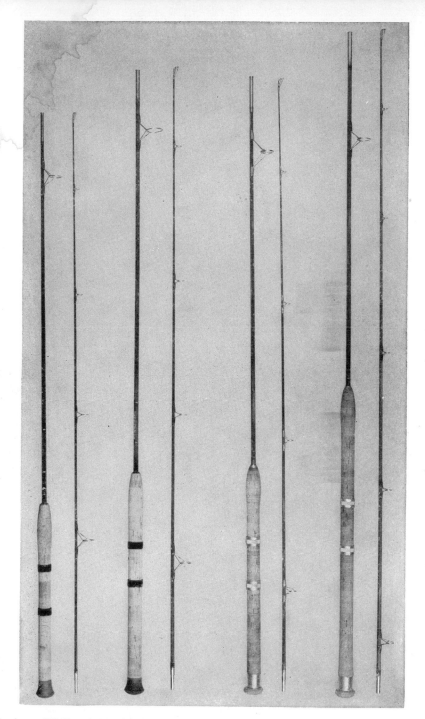

FOUR SPINNING RODS DESIGNED BY THE AUTHOR

(L to R) Seven-foot light and seven-and-a-half-foot medium action split-bamboo
rods made by the South Bend Bait Company; seven-and-a-half-foot medium
and eight-foot heavy action split-bamboo rods made by Traver Tackle, Inc.,
North Syracuse, N. Y.

This six-pound, four-ounce Eastern brook trout was taken by the author at the Sassamaskin-Vassal Fish and Game Reserve in Canada's Province of Quebec

The author's thirty-one pound, twelve-ounce rainbow trout, taken on spinning tackle at Lake Pend Oreille, Idaho, is the largest ever landed on light tackle

SPINNING GETS THE "BIG ONES"!

COMMENTS ON ROD GRIPS

It always has seemed to me that the grips on most American spinning rods are unsightly, awkward and inefficient. Many of them seem much too short and they are lacking in artistic and functional tapers. In trying to obtain rods that suited me, I have had dozens built according to my own desires. By process of testing and elimination, I finally arrived at a set of two split-bamboo rods primarily for fresh water use, and two glass-fiber rods especially suited for heavier salt water angling. This set of four, properly graduated in power, seems to provide an ideal weapon for everything from small pondfish to the largest surface-fighting oceanic tackle-busters.

I should like to call attention to the grips. Since they suit the needs of myself and of many others, perhaps we can take them as good examples. As in picture ("Four Spinning Rods"), the grips are longer than average. This helps to balance the rod for easier casting. It provides a rest against the forearm which makes it easier and less tiresome to manipulate the lure. The rubber butt cap and the longer grip allow the rod butt to be rested against the stomach while handling a fish. The swelled fore-end provides a most comfortable grip for the rod hand while reeling or during the run of a fish. Long experience has proved to me that these improvements are most helpful. Some of them have been adopted by other manufacturers.

The quality of the cork in the grip is important because cork relatively free from crevices and blemishes will not chip off as quickly as that usually found on the lower-priced rods. The rings should be sturdy, wide, and should fit the grip rather tightly. It is well to try the reel on the rod to see how tightly it fits, because an insecure union here may cause the reel to work loose when playing a fish. When a rod is new, one may have difficulty in forcing the rings over the foot of the reel, but if this can be done it is much better than to have the rings fit too easily. The reel foot ultimately will compress the cork, and the rings will shape themselves to the reel so that they will fit better after a little use.

If one cannot force the rings over the foot of the reel, it may be necessary to rub down the cork where the reel is to come against it. This can be done with a very fine flat file or with fine sandpaper. It should be done very cautiously, and then only as a last resort. If the rings become too loose, the reel can be secured to the rod with Scotch Electrical Tape, wound on in the form of a figure eight over and around the rings and the reel foot. (When fishing for big fish, this is a precaution I adopt frequently anyway.)

Anglers occasionally ask why locking reel seats are not used more commonly on spinning rods. One purpose of the long grip is to enable the user to attach the reel at any position along the grip that provides best action and greatest comfort. Actually, there is an ideal position on the grip for every reel, and this position may vary between one reel and another, for reasons which will be discussed. Foreign writers on spinning state that the long grip enables the angler to place the reel forward, to stiffen the rod slightly when using heavier lures, or rearward, to lengthen and lighten it for lighter lures. My opinion is that this makes very little difference and I think that the reel always should be placed in the position where greatest comfort and efficiency is obtained. I do not like locking reel seats because they are uncomfortable and unsightly on spinning rods. When the grip is properly turned to fit the rings, this method seems most satisfactory.

GUIDES AND TIP-TOPS

Suitable action in a spinning rod is of primary importance, but the selection and spacing of the guides is almost equally so. A rod with excellent action can be ruined by mistakes in choosing and applying the guides and even in the selection of the tip-top.

Guides for spinning rods are much larger than those used on other rods, because the line, casting off the reel in a succession of spirals, must be "guided" with minimum drag or obstruction as it travels swiftly forward. For this reason, all properly made guides are large, but especially the butt (or "gathering") guide, which is abnormally so in order to impede the flow of the line as little as possible. If we look through the guides on a spinning rod, they should give the appearance of a cone, each one being slightly smaller than the one behind it.

GUIDE SIZES

The French manufacturers make guides at least as good as any in the world. Following their example, a very few Americans also produce excellent ones. Figure 38 illustrates a partial set of guides as made by

FIGURE 38.

FRENCH-TYPE GUIDES AS MADE BY THE MILDRUM JEWEL COMPANY

the Mildrum Jewel Company, of East Berlin, Connecticut, which are made in sizes as shown on page 149.

Note that the rings of all spinning rod guides are set on supports which place the base of the butt guide about three quarters of an inch above the rod, and the smaller guides proportionately so. This offsetting has the purpose of preventing the line from slapping against the rod in casting.

Normally, spinning rod guides are made from stainless steel, over which is a hard plating of chrome. This

TABLE OF SIZES
FOR MILDRUM SPINNING ROD GUIDES

Identification Symbol	Outside Dia. of Ring in Inches	Distance from Center of Ring to Rod in Inches
SRA 48	2	1⅝
SRA 30	1¾₆	1⅜
SRA 24	1	1
SRA 17	¹¹⁄₁₆	¾
SRA 14	⁹⁄₁₆	⅝
SRA 12	⁷⁄₁₆	⁷⁄₁₆
SRA 10	¹³⁄₃₂	⅜
SRA 8	⁵⁄₁₆	⁹⁄₃₂
SRA 7	⁹⁄₃₂	¼
SRA 6	¼	¼

plating, when unbuffed, is almost imperceptibly rough to the touch, but so very slightly so that it can not harm the line. If the plating is not buffed or polished, it has a dull, silvery sheen which reflects less light and which therefore is preferable to the brightly polished (and less durably surfaced) method of finishing. Guides also can be obtained in finishes similar to gun metal, which is not as hard or as durable as the chrome — the decision between these largely being one of individual choice.

Agate guides can be obtained from importing firms such as Charles Garcia and Company, of New York City. Agate is similar to quartz in hardness and is harder than glass. The polished agate rings are set in German silver mountings, in such a way that they

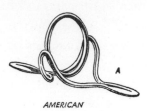

AMERICAN

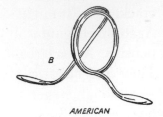

AMERICAN

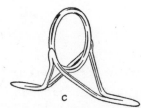

FRENCH GUIDE MADE BY MILDRUM

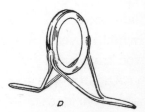

FRENCH OR GERMAN
AGATE-LINED GUIDE

GERMAN FOLDING
BUTT GUIDE

FIGURE 39.

TYPICAL SPINNING ROD GUIDES

can be turned by the fingers or with a pencil point with
slight difficulty. This nonrigid construction has the
double advantage of continuously offering new bearing surfaces to prevent the guide from being scored by
the line, and it also helps to prevent the agate from

cracking, as it might if it were more rigidly mounted. Agate-lined guides are very attractive and rather expensive. An accident will ruin them beyond repair. Their weight varies very little from solid metal guides — although, in general, they are inclined to be slightly heavier than the best of the stainless steel type. Porcelain-lined guides are similarly made; but the porcelain must be fused to the guide ring, an operation which is very expensive and which makes the guides too fragile for ordinary use.

Anglers who have tried all types of guides invariably consider the Mildrum or French type to be most practical. These guides combine a high degree of rigidity and hardness with a minimum of weight — three points almost vital to their purpose. There also are several American types which are designed somewhat differently, such as the ones shown in Figure 39. In some of them, the supports for the ring are curved inwardly, rather than being straight. This offers a tendency for the spiraling line to snub itself around the guide; a condition which can be most annoying. This fault, however, is due less to the construction of the guide than to where it is located. If the line has a tendency to wrap itself around the guide, the trouble can be remedied by shifting the guide to a better location. Excess vigor in casting may cause this also. Another type is in the form of a continuous looped wire which is chrome-plated. This has the advantage of being extremely light and of bending with the flexing of the rod, thereby eliminating stiff spots where the guides are bound to the rod. These guides are helpful especially on very light rods, but the gathering guide has a tendency to catch and snub the line between the double loop of wire when the loops separate slightly with the bending of the rod in casting.

The point is being made that a large butt guide is most necessary for long, easy casting. The large size of this guide makes it rather difficult to accommodate the rod, except in an ultra-wide tube. For this reason, folding guides, both with and without agate rings, can be obtained as shown in Figure 39. These are entirely practical except that their single support design allows the line occasionally to snub itself around the guide during a careless cast.

They accomplish very little except to allow the rod to be accommodated in a tube perhaps a half an inch narrower.

The weight of the tip-top must be reduced to an absolute minimum since its location on the tip of the rod multiplies any excess weight to the extent that it may ruin the action of the rod entirely. As an example, several years ago I helped a manufacturer to develop a spinning rod. After a lot of trouble in arriving at correct tapers, he sent me a sample which worked satisfactorily; and he kept an exact duplicate for a pilot model. A week or two after approving the rod, I happened to see his sample, wherein the action was very poor due to excess tip quiver. He stoutly maintained that the two rods were identical, yet it was easy to see that they were not. Finally we found out that a heavier tip-top had been used on the inferior one. When we alternated tip-tops, the good and the poor actions were transferred from one rod to the other. This illustrates the necessity of lightweight tip-tops and it should be added that their rings should be slightly larger than those used on fly rods, in order to

FIGURE 40.

SUPPORTED AND UNSUPPORTED TIP-TOPS FOR
SPINNING RODS

give the line greater freedom. Figure 40 shows a tip-top with side supports added for strength and a tip-top without side supports, similar to those used on fly rods. I like the latter type better because it is noticeably lighter. Without the side supports, the tip-top seems adequately strong. Another reason for the side supports is to prevent the line from wrapping itself around the ring; a situation which never has occurred in my experience.

FITTING GUIDES

When we buy a rod, the guides usually already have been fitted, but here is an easy way to check the

correctness of their locations, or to affix them properly
in rod building. It is most important first to locate the
butt guide, since this one has the leading responsibil-
ity for gathering the uncoiling line and for guiding it
through the others. To do this, let's first observe that
the axis of the spool of the spinning reel is not parallel
to the rod, but is tilted upward toward it slightly. Put
the reel on the rod about two thirds of the way forward
on the grip, and run the line through the tip-top. Hold
the line at the center of the front face of the reel spool,
and so place the butt guide that the line will pass

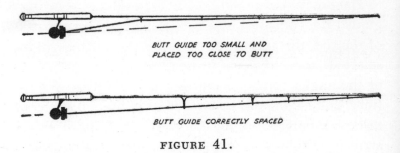

BUTT GUIDE TOO SMALL AND
PLACED TOO CLOSE TO BUTT

BUTT GUIDE CORRECTLY SPACED

FIGURE 41.

CORRECTLY AND INCORRECTLY SPACED BUTT
GUIDES

through it approximately at its center[1] and will continue on in a straight line through the tip-top as
shown in Figure 41. The guide chosen should be large

---

[1] Some anglers recommend that the line should pass through
the butt guide one third of its diameter nearer to the rod,
because even a fast uncoiling line tends to sag downward
somewhat when going through the butt guide.

enough, and should be offset sufficiently, to do this properly.

Spinning rods normally contain four guides in addition to the gathering guide and the tip-top, although the longer rods may accommodate five. They should be chosen as we have said, in properly graduated sizes, depending largely upon the size of the butt guide selected and upon the degree of lightness of the rod, so that they form the appearance of a cone when one looks through them. The line, when rigged as above, should pass through them all and remain straight.

The exact location of the guides (excluding the butt guide) depends on the length and degree of stiffness of the rod, the axis of the reel, the sizes of the guides selected and, to some extent, upon the judgment of the angler. In other words, guide spacing is arbitrary but in general follows a graduated pattern in distances between guides as shown in Figure 42. In arriving at this table of measurements, I checked several of the most successful rods I have had built and found that the spacing varies rather surprisingly. This is due largely to the "judgment of the angler," who should take into consideration the degree of lightness of the tip and should start his spacing a little closer for a light tip than for a stronger one in order that the strain may be distributed equitably along the rod.

Anglers who build their own rods often have a habit of temporarily fastening all guides in place with Scotch Electrical Tape and of testing the rod before

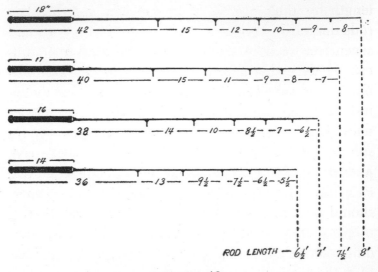

ROD LENGTH — 6½' 7' 7½' 8'

FIGURE 42.

APPROXIMATE LOCATIONS FOR SPINNING ROD
GUIDES (In inches)

permanently winding on the guides. This can be done
by asking someone else to cast with it while the rod's
owner observes the behavior of the line. Sometimes
several methods of guide spacing are tried before a
decision is made. For all ordinary angling, such ex-
perimentation seems unnecessary. The table in Figure
42 has been prepared in an effort to aid in solving
the problem quickly. This is an average of the spacing
of the several rods mentioned above, and I should repeat that liberties may be taken with it if the rod fit-
ter's judgment so advises.

We have noted that spinning rods have an ideal

length for their power. In fresh water split-bamboo rods this varies between eight feet for heavy rods and seven feet for light rods. Some of the glass-fiber rods can be somewhat shorter. I am convinced that ordinarily, and subject to the foregoing comments, longer rods are much handier and more efficient than shorter ones. The shorter ones now on the market are the result of misconceptions of manufacturers who have jumped to the unfortunate conclusion that spinning is "a form of bait casting" and that rods for the sport should be built accordingly. This could not be farther from the truth. My split-bamboo ultra-light spinning rods are seven feet long, and the only shorter ones than these are in the nature of miniatures which call for lines testing less than two pounds. Incidentally, even the lightest spinning-rod guides available as this is written are too heavy for the tips of most of the ultra-light rods. For these, I have used two or three fly-rod snake guides quite successfully, plus two or three of the lighter spinning-rod guides toward the butt. Such tiny tackle is a joy to use — but more about that in its proper place!

DETERMINING THE POWER OF RODS

In the past there has been no established method for determining the power of a rod and at the same time knowing immediately what sizes of lines and weights of lures should be used with it — not to mention the kinds of fishing for which it is best suited.

Because of this, anglers have known little about how to match their tackle when buying it. If they ultimately did find out, it was through their own experimental trials and errors. Manufacturers have built rods with only slight regard for their power, arbitrarily labeling them "light," "medium," or "heavy" — which certainly is not much help. In the next chapter I should like to advance some standards of my own

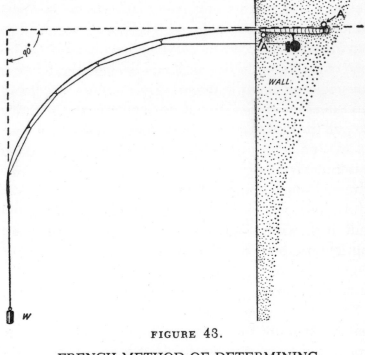

FIGURE 43.

FRENCH METHOD OF DETERMINING
THE POWER OF A SPINNING ROD

which may aid in solving this problem. As a preliminary to this, here are two methods for measuring rod power, as taken from the French. The French use the metric system, labeling their rods in grams. A four-hundred-gram rod, for example, is a rod of four hundred grams in power, which is about average.

Figure 43 shows the first of these two methods. The rod butt is secured between two nails or cleats (A) so that it is fastened horizontally with the entire stick extending free. A piece of line is fastened to the butt guide and is run through the guides and the tip-top. An increasing succession of weights are hooked to the end of the line until the tip of the rod is pulled down to an angle of ninety degrees, the line then becoming an extension of the vertical tip. The weight necessary to pull the tip to this right angle determines the power of the rod. This cannot harm a good rod if it is done carefully, but care should be taken to see that it is not strained much beyond this point.

An alternate method, which leads to the same result, is shown in Figure 44. The rod is fastened to an upright support by two straps (1) and (2) about eight inches apart on the grip so that it leans away from the support at an angle of about thirty degrees (XBC). A spring scale (A) is anchored two rod lengths from the butt (B) and the line from the rod is connected to it. The brake on the reel is tightened (with the anti-reverse lock on) and the reel is wound

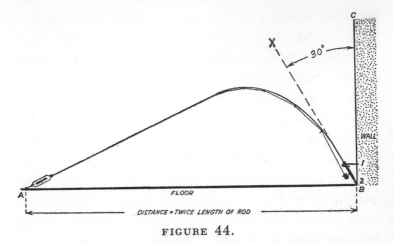

FIGURE 44.

ALTERNATE METHOD OF DETERMINING
THE POWER OF A SPINNING ROD

until the tip of the rod forms a continuation of the line.
The reading then on the spring scale is the power of
the rod.

In using these methods (derived from the "test
curve" of the English firm of Hardy Brothers, Ltd.)
the maximum weight of lures which the rod can handle is accepted to be one fiftieth (measured in grams)
of the power of the rod. Thus, a rod testing four hundred grams in power, for example, should accommodate lures weighing eight grams at a maximum. In
Europe, all rods are bought and sold on this basis.
Since Americans rarely use the metric system, this
method has not achieved prominence in this country,
although there is no reason why we cannot use it in
terms of ounces. The principle is a valuable one, and

we shall attempt to provide a similar and perhaps more acceptable substitute in the next chapter.

It should be noted that this book discusses rods in terms of power rather than of weight. Weight is highly misleading, due to the fittings, the grip, and to variations of the sticks themselves. When someone says that his spinning rod weighs six ounces, for example, this conveys only general information. When he says that the *power* of the rod is three pounds, we can tell instantly (See Figure 46, page 176) what strengths of lines and what weights of lures should be used with it and the kinds of fishing for which it is best suited. Consequently, it seems advisable to think of rods in terms of power and to forget almost entirely about weight.

GLASS FIBER RODS

Now that we have discussed the characteristics of spinning rods, let's touch briefly upon the materials from which they are made. Glass fiber rods seem to have invaded angling permanently, and many fishermen appear perplexed about what their advantages and limitations actually are. Glass fiber is a most valuable contribution to angling; but split bamboo has its advantages, too. I don't think I am a sentimental "diehard" when I say that I think and hope it always will have.

There has been a lot of secrecy in the manufacture

of rods of fibrous glass; but basically, the processes of making glass rods are much alike — in that fiber glass yarns are woven into fabrics in various ways and thicknesses, much as other cloths are made. The glass fiber cloth is impregnated with one type of phenolic resin or another and is rolled onto a tapered steel mandrel or core, whereon it is cured under definite degrees of heat and amounts of pressure for a specified length of time. Then the mandrel is removed and the tube (or blank) is surface-finished according to the manufacturer's judgment.

From this brief résumé we should note that the blanks of the various makers are not all alike, but vary somewhat in their characteristics depending upon many factors, including types of fabrics and resins used, the percentage of impregnation, the wall thickness, the length of the blank and the scheme of its taper. Anglers who use glass rods habitually become addicted to one make or another, because rods of this make have served them well and have earned their confidence. The casual fisherman need not concern himself too much over the technical details involved. He can test his prospective purchase in the manner we have described and, if it meets the standards which have been set, he should find his choice to be a wise one.

Glass rods have a quality which, to me, can best be defined by the word "guts." They need no varnishing and very little care. They will stand a lot of abuse, even in salt water fishing. They are strong, sturdy and extremely reliable. I am completely sold on them for heavy salt water spinning and I think they are ideal for the man who wants serviceable use, perhaps at the expense of some of the niceties which connoiseurs of fishing rods have been brought up to expect. Glass rods still are striving for perfection and they gradually seem to be approaching it. But if I am to judge by the many rods of all types which I have used, I must qualify my praise of glass fiber by saying that I have not yet found a light glass rod for fresh water fishing which provides the delicate, accurate action offered by the good examples of those made of split bamboo. Delicacy of action and pride of craftsmanship are, to me, very important factors in selecting light spinning rods. Here, I must join with many other anglers in feeling that split-bamboo rods still are supreme. The rough-and-tumble requirements of fishing are quite another matter.

SPLIT-BAMBOO RODS

Since the days when Hiram Leonard gave the split-bamboo rod its great eminence, the better examples of its craftsmanship have been treasured by anglers in the same way that a musician covets and admires a fine violin. In addition to the previous remarks about action, there are several inherent indications of quality which may be looked for in buying a rod of split bamboo. Most manufacturers fashion their sticks from six precisely machined triangular glued strips, but occasionally we find rods with four sides, or with five. Solid arguments can be advanced for each of these methods of construction, but all of them seem to boil down to a matter of individual preference. The number of strips in a rod is much less important than the quality of the rod itself. In this, there are several yardsticks which can aid our choice.

Examination of rods for action, for straightness, for choice of guides and for design of grip will narrow down the selection surprisingly. An excellent indication of high quality is the way the ferrules are made. Good ones are drawn to size from tubes of German silver. The female has a beautifully machined collar at its top, hard-soldered into place, and it has a German silver partition blocking the tube midway of its length to prevent moisture from entering and attacking the wood. The male usually is made of two pieces of tubing, one fitted and swedged over the other. The outside one forms a shoulder which permits the sticks being joined to be of equal diameters. The tip is closed by another solid hard-soldered partition, and thus is perfectly flat on the end. Cheap ferrules, on the other hand, are cupped and drawn from brass blanks and then are nickel- or chrome-plated. There is a rolled rim around the top of the female, for strength, and the tip of the male is rounded somewhat at the circumference. If we buy a low-priced rod, we cannot expect handmade German silver ferrules, but they are indicative of rods of the best quality.

Examine the nodes, which look like blemishes six inches or so apart along the strips. Those on each strip should be staggered from those on adjoining strips to keep them as far apart as possible for greater strength. Inspect the glue lines between the strips to see that they do not show and that there are no cracks in them. See that the ferrules are fitted to the wood, rather than the wood to the ferrules, since the latter method of construction, although being easier for the manufacturer, is weakening to the rod. Strips which have been darkened, indicating treatment by flame, are a sign of poor quality. Examine the grain lines in the wood, which should be straight along each strip, from end to end.

Split-bamboo rods essentially are handmade and, while these are only a few indications of craftsman-ship, they should suffice to tell which rods are good ones and which are less so. Craftsmanship can build into a rod a precise delicacy of action and an ideal distribution of power as yet unattained with similar products made by machine. Craftsmanship can make a fine rod seem like a living thing, instantly responsive to the skill of the angler.

The practicability of varying the tapers of rods of split bamboo, thus making it possible to distribute power or strength as desired, allows a much wider range and more delicate adjustment of actions in these rods than is possible in those of glass fiber. The processes of making glass-fiber rods call for straight tapers, which restricts them considerably in their varieties of actions. Thus, among rods in the lighter strengths particularly, much more delicacy and precision can be enjoyed with rods of split bamboo than with those made of fiber glass.

METAL RODS

Although many metal rods for spinning have been made from tubing of steel and from copper alloys, none of these attempts seem to have approached the success of rods made from glass fiber or from split bamboo. The competition of glass fiber in the field of less expensive rods has come so closely to driving rods of metal from the market that it seems superfluous to attempt to add information about them.

SELECTING THE ROD FOR THE JOB

One properly chosen spinning outfit may suffice for anglers who do not roam too far afield for their fishing. But the tackle requirements of the many types of fresh and salt water angling are so varied that, if we are to enjoy them comprehensively, it is advisable to own two spinning outfits of different power, or perhaps even more. To pick the right rod for the job, we must know what strengths of lines and what weights of lures we want to use with it. We should select the proper combination to allow us to cast as far as we wish, and to afford whatever power is necessary to handle the fish we intend to seek under the conditions in which they are found. Since all this is a subject deserving rather detailed explanation, the next chapter is devoted to a discussion of tackle for your rod.

CHAPTER SEVEN

How to Match Spinning Tackle

NO FLY-FISHERMAN who understands how to make his rod cast its line and fly far and true would think of using a line which does not bring out the power of his rod, because a line which does not match its rod is clumsy and ineffectual. In fact, the expert fly rod angler tests his tackle until he knows exactly what type and weight of line he should use, exactly how long his leaders should be, and just how they should be tapered to present wet fly, dry fly, streamer or nymph properly to the fish.

If a similar high regard for the niceties of matching tackle does not exist among spinning anglers, it is because they have not yet acquired sufficient experience to realize its value. If those who read these pages have difficulty in making long casts easily and accurately, a bit of attention paid to the proper mating of rod, line and lures should go far toward solving the problem.

In fly-fishing, the line must have correct and correctly distributed weight to carry out the relatively weightless fly. In spinning, the line must be as light as advisable — because it is the weight of the lure, and the power of the rod to cast it, which pulls the line from the fixed spool reel. It is quite obvious that a given lure will cast farther with a lighter line than with a heavier one. It is equally obvious that a lure which is too heavy may cause too light a line to break, or it may damage too light a rod. If the lure is not heavy enough, it will not bring out the power of the rod and it will not carry the line to the expected distance.

There is, therefore, a definite relationship between the strengths of lines and the weights of lures which should be used with rods of any given size or power. There is a definite relationship between the size or power of the rod and the kind of fishing in which we ordinarily will expect it to help us. As we have seen in the last chapter, to get full enjoyment and best results from spinning, it is highly important to select a good spinning rod powerful enough (but not too powerful) for its intended work. Now to it must be matched a line (or lines) suitable in strength, and a set of lures neither too heavy nor too light to bring out its action to fullest advantage. It is true that spinning tackle is noted for its ability to make long, easy, accurate casts, but these qualities are in direct relationship to the care its owner takes in assembling lines and lures which are suitable for his rod. The expert spinning angler is just as fussy about all this as is the expert fly caster — and just as rightly so.

The point has been brought out that spinning-rod manufacturers have made little effort to tell anglers very much about the power of the rods they intend them to buy. They have not fully realized the importance of this, and no logical standards have been set to guide them. When no standards exist, it is up to somebody to devise them.

The most intelligent attempt in this direction which I know of is a development by Bob Cowell, an experienced and inquiring spinning angler who is proprietor of a progressive tackle shop in Brookline, Massachusetts. His method of solving the problem stems from the French system of determining rod power, which has been described. To this he has added a formula for deciding upon the sizes of lines best suited for any rod, and upon the weights of lures which can be cast to maximum advantage with the tackle. He also has come upon a very sensible method of adjusting the reel brake safely for the strength of line involved. I have undertaken to simplify and to amend his formula somewhat, and I shall try to explain the result in the hope that it will be as helpful to others as it has been to me.

If the manufacturer does not give the angler a true index of the power of his rod, it behooves the fisherman or the dealer to determine it, because this is the information which so easily reveals the strengths of lines and the weights of lures which should be used with the rod in question.

THE BATES-COWELL METHOD OF
MATCHING TACKLE

This method, as shown in Figure 45, is similar to the French method of determining rod power except that the rod is held by the angler at an angle which varies slightly, depending upon the degree of stiffness of the rod. A spring scale with a large dial is used, such as is frequently seen in grocery stores. This is fastened near the floor, and a fairly heavy line is connected to it and run through a large screw-eye or small pulley to give the line a direct downward pull. A swivel or snap swivel is attached to it so that the line from the reel may be connected easily.

The angler stands three rod-lengths away from the dial, with tackle rigged, and tightens the brake screw of the reel enough to lock the spool. He also engages the anti-backwind device to keep the reel from turning backward. He holds the rod at a forty-five degree angle for stiff rods, and somewhat higher for more limber ones (about fifty-five degrees from the horizontal for medium rods and about seventy degrees for softer ones), to compensate for the degree of softness of the tip. The variation in this angle is designed to bring out the maximum power of each type of rod.

In this position the angler cranks the reel until the rod tip bends enough to form a continuation of the line; that is, to remove entirely the angle between line and rod tip. He must experiment somewhat in arriv-

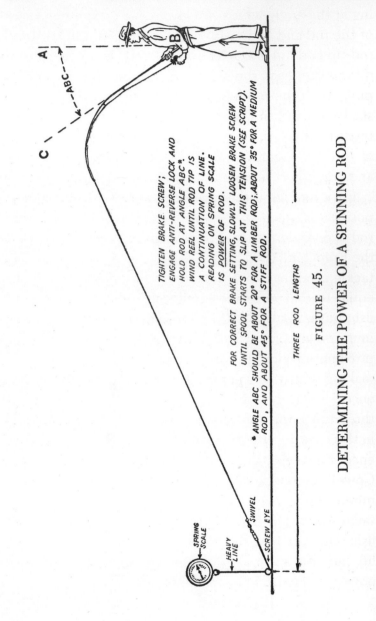

THREE ROD LENGTHS

TIGHTEN BRAKE SCREW;
ENGAGE ANTI-REVERSE LOCK AND
HOLD ROD AT ANGLE ABC*.
WIND REEL UNTIL ROD TIP IS
A CONTINUATION OF LINE.
READING ON SPRING SCALE
IS POWER OF ROD.

FOR CORRECT BRAKE SETTING, SLOWLY LOOSEN BRAKE SCREW
UNTIL SPOOL STARTS TO SLIP AT THIS TENSION (SEE SCRIPT).

* ANGLE ABC SHOULD BE ABOUT 20° FOR A LIMBER ROD; ABOUT 35° FOR A MEDIUM
ROD, AND ABOUT 45° FOR A STIFF ROD.

SPRING SCALE

HEAVY LINE

SWIVEL

SCREW EYE

A

ABC

C

B

FIGURE 45.

DETERMINING THE POWER OF A SPINNING ROD

ing at the angle which brings out the maximum power of the rod and he must be sure that the angle between rod tip and line has been eliminated. Under these conditions, he reads the scale to determine the amount of pull which the rod has provided. The tackle should be slackened and brought up to this tension three or four times to check the accuracy of the reading. The power of the rod is considered to be the reading in pounds and fraction of a pound multiplied by three.

For example, if the pulling power of the rod in this position is exactly one pound, the actual power of the rod is considered to be three pounds. This varies from the French method for the following reason. When the tackle is under the tension above described, it is about equal to that normally employed in handling a large fish, but is far less than the breaking strength or maximum power of the rod. A strong jerk upward will approximately double the reading on the spring scale, making it in this instance about two pounds. Experience shows that it would require a force of about three times the spring-scale reading, or three pounds in this case, to utilize all the power of the rod. A difference between the French method and the Bates-Cowell method is that in the latter the angler is determining rod power from a practical standpoint, in the same manner as he would use this power in playing a fish. He can feel the rod's action in his hands and he can use accurate judgment in deciding upon its power, guided by the standard set.

When we have arrived at a very accurate reading of the spring scale and thus have determined the power of the rod, we also have learned the theoretical line strength which will match most safely the rod which has been tested. This, in pounds, is the same as the power of the rod; that is, a rod with a power of three pounds can be equipped most efficiently with a line testing three pounds in breaking strength.

Let's consider the logic of this. The angler in Figure 45 is in a position which indicates in practice that he is exerting pull on a fish equal to the normal pulling power of the rod. Yet we have seen that if the fish is a powerful one and if he elects to shake strongly or to start a quick run, the spring scale may indicate approximately twice the normal pulling power, or two thirds of the theoretical maximum strength of the rod and line. This still leaves us a reserve of one third of the line's theoretical maximum strength, which should be safe for the tackle involved. We also have another factor of safety in that the knot which secures the lure usually is less strong than the line itself.

Now comes the problem of arriving at a logical range of line strengths, the minimum of which should prove safe with careful handling and the maximum of which should allow relatively long casts with the strongest line advisable; that is, a line such as might be called for in fishing in a heavy current or near lily pads, rocks, stumps or similar obstructions.

Since it has been noted that a fish may exert strain equal to twice the normal pulling power of the rod, or two thirds of the theoretically ideal line strength, it would not seem safe to reduce the theoretical minimum by more than 25 per cent of the calculated ideal line strength for the rod in question. The maximum strength is more arbitrary. The higher we go, the less distance we will obtain from the cast. So let's select a reasonable maximum of 50 per cent greater than the theoretically ideal line strength, realizing that, in choosing this maximum, the rod is protected by the correct brake setting to be described. This gives us a 75 per cent range — such as, for the rod with the theoretical power of three pounds, from 2.25 to 4.50 pounds — in the line's breaking strength. We may use the minimum for long casts with the lighter lures, or the maximum for exerting greatest power on the larger fish when they are near obstructions. If we use lines testing less than the minimum, we run into constant danger of breaks. If we use lines testing more than the maximum, we unduly penalize ourselves on casting distance and we use lines far too strong for the power of the rod. In fact, for all normal purposes, common sense would seem to restrict us to a range between the minimum and the ideal theoretical line strengths, as shown in Figure 46.

Now, it may be well to consider the element of individual judgment in using this method. A spring scale is a rough measure at best, so the angler must not

Rod Size	Pulling Power of Rod in Pounds	Actual Power of Rod in Pounds	Theoretical Ideal Line Strength in Pounds	Theoretical Max. and Min. Line Strengths in Pounds	Recommended Range of Lure Weights in Ounces	Ideal Lure Weight in Oz.	Recommended Type of Reel
(A)	½	1½	1.50	1.125 to 2.250	.112 to .225	.150	Light
(B)	1	3	3.00	2.250 to 4.500	.225 to .450	.300	Light or Medium
(C)	1½	4½	4.50	3.375 to 6.750	.337 to .675	.450	Medium
(D)	2	6	6.00	4.500 to 9.000	.450 to .900	.600	Medium
(E)	2½	7½	7.50	5.625 to 11.25	.562 to 1.12	.750	Medium or Heavy
(F)	3	9	9.00	6.750 to 13.50	.675 to 1.35	.900	Heavy
(G)	3½	10½	10.50	7.875 to 15.75	.787 to 1.57	1.05	Heavy
(H)	4	12	12.00	9.000 to 18.00	.900 to 1.80	1.20	Heavy or Extra Capacity
(I)	4½	13½	13.50	10.12 to 20.25	1.01 to 2.02	1.35	Heavy or Extra Capacity
(J)	5	15	15.00	11.25 to 22.50	1.12 to 2.25	1.50	Heavy or Extra Capacity

TYPE OF FISHING FOR WHICH TACKLE IS BEST SUITED:

Rod Size "A": Ultra-light Casting in Open Water with Little or no Current
" " "B": Light Casting in Ponds, Lakes or Streams in Unobstructed Water
" " "C": Pond or Lake Fishing Near Obstructions, or All Average Stream Fishing
" " "D": Heavy Pond, Lake or Stream Fishing, or Light Salt Water Angling
" " "E": Extra-heavy Pond, Lake or Fast Water Fishing, or Light Salt Water Angling
" " "F": Fast Water Fishing for Big Fish, or Medium Salt Water Angling
" " "G": Extra-heavy Fresh Water Fishing; Medium Salt Water Angling Near Obstructions
" " "H": Heavy Salt Water Fishing or Average Surf Casting
" " "I": Heavy Salt Water Fishing Near Obstructions, or Heavy Surf Casting
" " "J": Heaviest Salt Water Angling for All Surface Fighting Fish

FIGURE 46.

THEORETICAL TABLE FOR MATCHING TACKLE

*When Fish Lie Deep in Fast Water, Small, Weighted Spinning
Lures Are Especially Successful*

*A Spinning Angler Lands an Eight-Pound Steelhead on Oregon's
Wide and Swift Deschutes River . . .*

. . . and Brings the Steelhead Back to Camp for Dinner

be careless in testing the pulling power of his rod, since any error he makes is multiplied by three. Manufacturers (especially of American nylon monofilament) frequently underestimate line strengths, oftentimes by as much as 25 per cent. I have used lines (usually braided) where the published strength was badly overestimated. Foreign monofilaments usually are more correctly labeled. These factors introduce an element which calls for the use of judgment by the angler. And they may not consider adequately the fact that the line later may become weakened in use. In any event, we have reached a standard method of determining rod power and line strength which is far better than sheer guesswork, and which allows for a reasonable factor of safety. It would be a simple matter for spinning tackle dealers to install such a spring scale in their stores, so anglers could check the power of the rods they intend to buy.

Now, let's decide upon the proper weights of lures to cast with the rod and with the lines we have selected. The weights of lures, in terms of the casting strain exerted upon the rod, are influenced by the air-resistance of the lures in question. Smooth, streamlined lures will remain in the recommended range, shown, in Figure 46. The others, dressed with hair or feathers, or in air-resistant shapes, must be considered as being a bit heavier than they are, because they put a greater strain on the rod. Nevertheless, the ideal weight and the recommended range shown in the table should be of aid until use with the rod in question establishes weights more nearly correct. It is easy in casting to notice which lures are too light to bring out the power of the rod and which are so heavy that they strain and deaden the action of the rod unduly. Both the ideal weight and the recommended range which we have arrived at in Figure 46 are set at one tenth of the same figures, expressed in ounces, as the theoretical ideal and maximum and minimum line-strengths expressed in pounds.

For example, with the rod having a pulling power of one pound, and an actual power of three pounds, we have determined that the ideal line-strength is three pounds and the correct range of line strengths is from 2.250 to 4.500 pounds. The theoretically ideal lure-weight for this tackle would be one tenth of three pounds (expressed in ounces), or three tenths of an ounce, and the range of lure weights would be from .225 to .450 ounces, or approximately from just less than a quarter to just less than a half an ounce. Of course, we can go as much lighter in lure weight as we wish, at the expense of casting distance. We also can go somewhat heavier if we feel that the added weight will not overtax the rod.

We may note that this Bates-Cowell method, reached independently of the French method, agrees very accurately with it in determining lure weights. The French method was developed for rods of split bamboo, but tests with both methods indicate that the rules established work equally well for rods of glass fiber, since the basis is rod power, regardless of the material from which the rod is made.

However, glass fiber is a more rugged material and does not "take a set" under abnormal strain, as does split bamboo. Glass-fiber rods remain straight under stress until they break. Therefore, while the lure weights given are correct for both types of rods, it should be safe to use slightly heavier lures with glass rods than this table calls for, if the rod in question seems to handle them efficiently.

CHOICE OF REEL SIZES

The choice of the proper size of reel is not a critical one, except for the functional elements of quality which have been discussed. Spinning reels for light tackle should be correspondingly light in weight or small in size to balance the rod comfortably. Those for heavier tackle should be larger and sturdier and should contain at least as much line as the angler thinks he will need.

I have listed below a score or so of the best-known reels identified by their weights and capacities as "light," "medium," "heavy" and "extra-capacity" to indicate the range of sizes available for use with the table in Figure 46. While these reels include many of the most popular, the elimination of others does not necessarily mean that they are less well recommended. Since new reels constantly are coming on the market, it is nearly impossible to include all of the good ones on a list such as this:

Light Reels	Alcedo Micron	Spinnette
	Staro	(Langley)
Medium Reels	Alcedo 2CS[1]	Luxor Supreme[1]
	Altex No. 2	Mastereel
	Ambidex	Mitchell
	Cap	Orvis
	Centaure "River"	Fix
	Heddon Manual	Ocean City 300
	Record	Ru Sport
	Luxor	Martin
Heavy Reels	Centaure	Ru Mer
	Beachcomber	
Heavy Extra	Luxor Mer Surf	Ru Atlantic
Capacity Reels	Atlantis	

The line capacity of any orthodox spinning reel should be more than adequate for every fresh water purpose. If the reel is to be used in salt water, one should be selected which holds the desired amount of line.

THE COWELL METHOD OF BRAKE ADJUSTMENT

The proper adjustment of a spinning reel brake has been a problem which previously has been solved entirely by individual judgment, without any standard

[1] These more correctly could be classed as "Medium-Heavy."

to guide it. Anglers habitually set their brakes too tightly on the one hand and too loosely on the other, resulting in broken lines and less sport in the first instance, and inadequate hooking and holding power in the second. It is important to arrive at a happy median between these two extremes because proper brake adjustment is excellent insurance for success in spinning.

Bob Cowell has determined one of the easiest methods imaginable. It ties in with the Bates-Cowell method of matching tackle and precludes that the angler has selected a line in the proper strength range for his rod, as this method advises.

The tackle is rigged and held by the angler as we have described in Figure 45. The brake is screwed down so that the reel spool will not slip when the rod is raised to the tension which gives it proper pulling power. In this position, the brake screw is loosened very slowly and gradually until it just begins to give way. To test the accuracy of this adjustment, when the rod is arched as described (so that the line forms a continuation of the rod tip) the brake should not slip but, if the angle backs away (simulating the run of a fish), the brake should release line immediately. This is the correct adjustment for ordinary fishing, but of course it can be changed if the angler prefers to do so.

With this setting, the rod can be arched properly with the brake set tightly enough to manage the fish.

If the fish exerts a stronger pull than this, the brake will slip and allow the reel to give line, but not otherwise. The entire combination provides the right line strength and lure weight for the rod, with the brake correctly set for maximum efficiency.

I have suggested that the angler first try this method on the spring scale so that he can determine for himself the hooking power his tackle will exert when he strikes a fish and the resistance it will provide when the fish is making a run. At this setting it will be observed that when a fish takes line from the spool, the line is only being called upon for one third of its strength. When a fish strikes, jerks or starts a run, the pull on the line temporarily may be about two thirds of its strength. This brake adjustment, therefore, leaves us a factor of safety of at least one third of the line's strength, allowing safe leeway for the lesser strength of the terminal knot and for errors in judgment.

In the position of the rod to which the brake has been adjusted, the rod tip forms a continuation of the line. Before fishing, without a spring scale or anything else, the brake can be adjusted similarly merely by hooking the lure to anything convenient and duplicating the arch of the rod at a distance of three rod-lengths from where the lure is fastened. The brake is first screwed down, and then, with the rod under the above tension, the screw gradually is released until it just begins to slip when the angler backs away. In

correctly setting the brake by this means it is important not to do so by jerking the rod, since this does not
provide as accurate an adjustment as is obtained by
backing away from the lure.

The method provides maximum safe power for the
tackle and is extremely simple and quick to use. Once
the brake has been set by this method, anglers rarely
should disturb it. If added tension is needed temporarily, they can use the reel hand or the forefinger of
the rod hand for added braking when necessary (as
will be described in Chapter Eight, on casting).

Every once in a while it is the good fortune of all
anglers to hook into an abnormally big fish. Skill and
luck play big parts in landing him, but correctly selected and properly matched tackle, well cared for
and accurately adjusted, plays a vital part also. All
together, these advantages contribute to a feeling of
confidence in the fisherman. And confidence is an aw-
fully important thing in angling!

CHAPTER EIGHT

Suggestions for Accurate Casting

ON ONE OF THOSE BALMY spring days which seem created especially for fishermen I stopped to watch the occasional shimmering leaps of the rainbow trout as they attempted to ascend the white cascade of the power dam. Then I walked downstream to the riffles of the wide river, to see if I could tempt them with a spinning lure.

Around the bend, a fisherman stood at the tail of the pool, fumbling with a spinning outfit, obviously very new. He filled the air with muttered curses as he tried to adjust his line, which was much too loosely wound on his reel. Finally, he attempted a prodigious cast, combining the wind-up of a baseball pitcher with the full-arm swing of a mule driver beating his contrary beast into action. The lure sailed gracefully into some bushes and a few coils of line, prematurely pulled off the reel by the fisherman's intense exertion, tangled themselves in the gathering guide of his rod. When the man returned from finding his lure and sat down to unsnarl the mess, he unburdened a tale of most unnecessary woe.

"Just bought this thing," he apologized. "Been

reading an article on spinning and the chap who wrote it said it was pretty easy to learn how. Just a few minutes of practice, he said, would teach me all I need to know to go out and catch fish. So I parted with sixty bucks for this miserable outfit and I have stood here all morning getting nervous indigestion and piling trouble upon trouble. If I could find that so-and-so of a magazine writer, I'd wrap this silly outfit around his neck."

He glanced at my tackle. "I see you fell for it, too!" he said. ". . . Gee, lookit! Did you see that big rainbow roll?"

To make a long story short, this new acquaintance and I fished together for the remainder of the day. It was not until darkness had fallen and we were having a glass of ale at the local tavern that he discovered it was I who had been the instigator of his difficulties. By that time, he had learned many rudiments of spinning which it would have been better for him to have absorbed before going on the stream. He had taken two nice rainbow trout and "wouldn't have missed the whole thing for a million dollars!" What little he previously had read evidently had gone in one eye and out of the other; but the story illustrates anew that, while spinning may be relatively easy, it is more sensible to learn whatever is possible in advance, and thus insure greater enjoyment of the relatively short time we can spend on lake or stream.

Even anglers who are fairly old hands at spinning

sometimes fail to handle their tackle so that they can enjoy easy accuracy with it. Some of them, for example, turn the reel handle to close the pickup to stop the cast, when the forefinger can control line and lure more easily and accurately. Some of them cast with the line tightly held against the rod grip, thus delaying release of the lure and further impairing accuracy. Errors such as this are due to lack of instruction, or to improper instruction — and they damage the enjoyment and efficiency we can derive from spinning gear. Since accurate and easy casting is so very simple, and so very important, let's mentally assemble our outfit and go down to an imaginary dock to make a few practice casts.

THE IMPORTANCE
OF FOREFINGER CONTROL

The most important element in the ease and accuracy of casting is to learn to slow down the line or to stop it by using the forefinger of the rod hand. The forefinger acts as an auxiliary brake when needed. The rod and reel must be so held that the forefinger can be brought into quick and easy contact with the front face of the reel spool, as shown in illustration "Casting Positions." It will help to study these illustrations and to keep them in mind until forefinger control becomes instinctive.

Since the legs of the various reels are curved differently, and since fingers vary in length, one must decide how many fingers should be held ahead (and how many behind) of the reel leg in order that the forefinger can make proper contact with the front face of the reel spool. Some reels and hands make it most comfortable to place only the forefinger ahead. Others call for two fingers, or three. There are reels with radically curved legs so designed that all four fingers should be placed ahead. The majority of reels are made for putting two fingers in front of, and two behind, the leg, a grasp which usually is most comfortable and efficient. Regardless of the way the reel is designed, it is a matter of only a minute or two to decide the proper grip. That is the one to use with the reel in question every time, without change. The position of the tip of the forefinger against the front face of the reel spool decides the matter.

NOTES ON FOREFINGER CONTROL

Let's stop for a minute to consider how important this is. When we get ready to make a cast, the reel cup and pickup arm are rotated clockwise by the fingers of the left hand (which are in the position shown in illustration 3) until the roller is nearest to the rod grip. This makes it easy to pick up the line over the *tip* of the forefinger, after which the left hand then turns the cup and pickup counterclockwise until it is in its downward position, where it is free of the line and may be opened preparatory to making a cast.

The important thing is to pick up the line with the

tip of the forefinger, which is partly crooked so that, by extending it slightly, the line will slide off. If the line were picked up farther back on the forefinger (such as in the cleft of the joint) the line would not slide off as easily and thus would delay its release, impairing the accuracy of the cast.

Since this element of forefinger control has such a decided effect upon accuracy, it may be well to rehearse the two "Do's" and the two "Don't's" upon which it depends. *Do* place the line as near the *tip* of the forefinger as possible without allowing it to slide off. *Do* keep the forefinger extended as far as possible, still allowing it to hold the line. *Don't* curl the forefinger excessively, or hold the line against the rod grip. *Don't* place the line farther back on the forefinger than necessary; especially not in the finger joint.

With this in mind, let's see how easy it is to make a practice cast! The line is over the forefinger's tip and the pickup has been backed off to a downward position, out of the way, and has been opened.

Using the wrist only, bring the rod tip downward to the right. Using the wrist only, sweep the rod upward and forward, extending the forefinger instantly as the rod is stopped, pointing over the target. Extending the forefinger causes the line to slide off it and allows the lure to soar out toward its objective.

Now, let's stop the lure. All we need to do is to touch the front face of the reel spool with the forefinger. This snubs the line and arrests the lure instantly in flight. In actual fishing, we will stop the lure just as it is about to touch the water, or when we think it is going astray during a bad cast. Right now, the important thing is to see how quickly we can stop it. Forefinger control and a bit of practice allows the angler to arrest his lure within inches of the far bank of a stream, a log, a rock or any other spot he wishes to reach, but not to touch. How much more accurate and easy this is than fumbling with the reel handle in order to stop the cast with the pickup arm of the reel! In casting, let's forget that the reel handle and pickup arm exist. We don't need them!

Suppose we wish to slow down the lure in flight, preparatory to stopping it just as it reaches its objective? When the cast is going out, the forefinger is extended — and we leave it in that position until it is needed. To slow down the lure, all that is necessary is to bring the forefinger toward the reel spool, allowing the uncoiling line to slap against it. The slapping of the line against the forefinger brakes the line and slows the flight of the lure. The closer the forefinger is brought toward the reel spool, the greater is the braking effect.

Let's assume that we have made the cast and have stopped the line with the forefinger just as the lure touches the water. At this instant a fish takes the lure. What do we do? The forefinger is against the reel spool after the cast has been stopped, and it is kept there to keep more line from uncoiling from the reel.

When the fish strikes, all we need to do is to raise the rod tip to hook him. The forefinger is in control of the line, and we do not have to put the line under control of the reel until we are ready to do so. This, of course, is done with a partial turn of the reel handle, causing the pickup arm to revolve and to take the line from the forefinger.

Now for another instance of forefinger control! Let's assume that we are casting cross-stream into a current and that we will want to release line from time to time to allow the lure to travel downstream. We have made the cast and the line is being controlled from being released because of the pressure of the forefinger on the face of the spool. We keep the forefinger in that position while the lure sinks and swings with the current. When we want to release more line, we let up on the pressure of the forefinger, allowing a coil or more to escape from the reel as slowly or as rapidly as desired. When enough line has been released and we want to reel it in, a partial turn of the reel handle will put the line under control of the reel again.

The forefinger also can act as an auxiliary brake when necessary. If a fish is taking line from the reel too rapidly, perhaps due to the brake being too lightly set, added braking power can be provided by forefinger pressure on the revolving reel spool. Such braking is comfortable only temporarily. When longer or more intense pressure is needed, it can be given by cradling the reel with the palm of the left hand, as shown in Picture 5 of "Casting Positions." These methods allow instantaneous auxiliary braking to any degree that the angler desires. They put his fish under as perfect control as the strength of line will allow. It is important not to underestimate this braking power, since too firm pressure can lock the reel and snap the line.

While we are accomplishing all this with forefinger control, we are gaining other advantages also. By stopping the flow of the line just *before* the lure touches the water, we allow the lure to travel an additional foot or two to take all unnecessary slack out of the line. When the slack is removed, the lure also straightens out, assuring that it will land hook-forward, thus not catching on the line and fouling the cast. This method keeps all slack out of the line, both on the reel spool and in the air. It gives continual control of line and lure and makes the angler ready to hook a fish instantly, regardless of when he strikes!

Forefinger control of line, of lure and of brake is so easy and so instantaneous that supreme accuracy in casting depends only upon the ability of the angler to master the method. Forefinger control makes it possible to drop a lure within inches of its target. It allows us to stop lures instantly, or to slow them down at will. It allows the paying out of line from the reel as desired, to make the fishing of runs and riffles more resultful. It acts as an auxiliary brake when needed. It is vital in keeping the tight line so necessary in spinning. It eliminates fumbling with the reel handle and the pickup arm completely. It is the greatest secret of perfect casting and of gaining maximum success in spinning.

When forefinger control has become instinctive, more than half of the difficulties of casting are over. It only remains for the angler to know a few simple ways of making the various types of casts. I shall take them up in order of their importance to me, describing the good and bad points of each. One may be ideal for one occasion and another for another. No one offers a sure solution for every problem of reaching a target under the many restrictions which nature imposes.

THE SIDE CAST

I find myself using this one somewhat more frequently than others because it excels in getting distance and because it makes the lure travel in a relatively low trajectory, putting minimum "belly" in the line. As such, it is particularly good for casting on windy days. Its disadvantage lies in the fact that (unlike the overhead cast) the angler must cast both in a horizontal and in a vertical plane. Getting proper altitude and distance for the flight of the lure is easy. Getting the lure to travel in the exact direction we want it to go depends entirely on instantaneously accurate release of the line; a factor in which forefinger control is of paramount value.

Turn cup to bring pickup roller nearest to rod grip. Pick line off pickup roller with tip of forefinger.

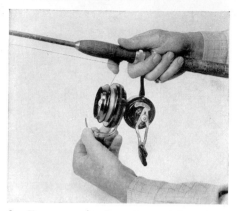

2. *Turn cup backward so pickup is in downward position and line is disengaged from it. Open pickup arm*

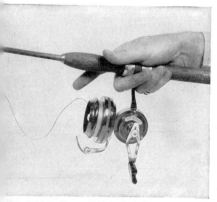

As cast is made, point forefinger toward target, thus releasing line and lure

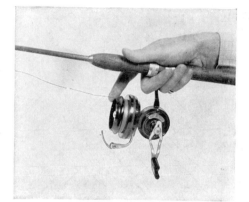

4. *Lure can be slowed down by lowering forefinger toward reel spool; can be stopped by touching forefinger to reel spool*

n handling fish during runs, engage ntireverse lock and provide added raking pressure when necessary by pplying finger and thumb of left and lightly to reel spool

CASTING POSITIONS

Accurate Casting with Spinning Tackle may be Learned Quickly
But it takes study and practice to absorb all the intricacies of spinning

Reel in the lure until it is about six inches from the rod tip. This is the proper position for the lure in the first three types of casts to be mentioned. One can vary this very slightly depending on the type of lure used, but if the lure is reeled in too close to the rod tip the result is to choke the action of the rod and to restrict the angler somewhat in the distance he should obtain.

In this cast, remember to use the wrist almost exclusively, the forearm only slightly, and the upper arm not at all. Excess exertion does more harm than good. Try keeping the elbow close to the body and not moving it during the cast.

Face the target and point the rod toward and slightly above it — at an angle of about forty-five degrees above the horizontal if maximum distance is to be attempted. Following the sketches in Figure 47, and using the wrist primarily, snap the rod slightly downward and to the right. This will cause the rod to flex. Using the maximum flexing of the rod (to get maximum power), sweep the rod forward and slightly upward in the same path, extending the forefinger to release the lure at the instant that the rod is stopped pointing over the target. The secret of accuracy in this cast is the proper release of the line. If it is released too late, the cast will travel too far to the left; if released too early, it will travel too far to the right. To make the lure travel a relatively short distance, the cast can be started downward from the side, thus flexing the rod to a minimum extent. In practice, it is well to try for accuracy, rather than for distance. Distance depends upon the power put into the cast, upon

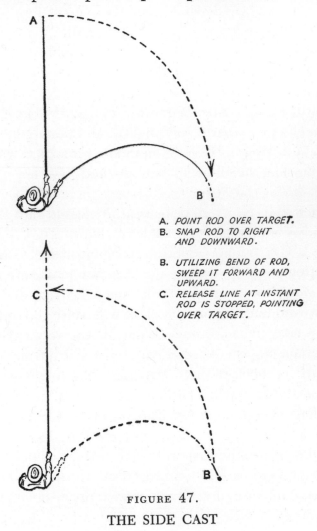

A. POINT ROD OVER TARGET.
B. SNAP ROD TO RIGHT
   AND DOWNWARD.

B. UTILIZING BEND OF ROD,
   SWEEP IT FORWARD AND
   UPWARD.
C. RELEASE LINE AT INSTANT
   ROD IS STOPPED, POINTING
   OVER TARGET.

FIGURE 47.

THE SIDE CAST

the relative weight and lack of air resistance of the lure, upon the height of the trajectory of the lure, and upon the relative lightness of the line being used.

THE OVERHEAD CAST

This allows the lure to travel in a single vertical plane, and therefore it is more conducive to accuracy than is the side cast. If one wishes to drop a lure into a small circle at an average distance, this type of cast is a good one to use. Its disadvantage lies primarily in the fact that the lure travels in a relatively high trajectory, thus causing a larger belly in the line, which may be disadvantageous on windy days. This can be controlled somewhat by the angle at which the lure is released, by the power put into the cast, and by stopping the flow of line just before the lure reaches the target.

As shown in Figure 48, this cast is started as before, by pointing the rod toward and slightly above the target, keeping the elbow close to the side of the body. Snap the rod upward, stopping it at a position of about twelve o'clock. Bring it forward immediately in order to keep maximum bend in the rod, and release the lure as the rod is stopped pointing toward and slightly over the target. The forefinger should stop the outward flow of line a bit sooner in this cast than in the side cast, in order to remove the excess belly in the line.

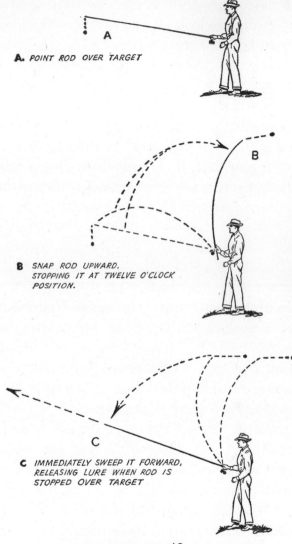

A. POINT ROD OVER TARGET

B SNAP ROD UPWARD,
STOPPING IT AT TWELVE O'CLOCK
POSITION.

C IMMEDIATELY SWEEP IT FORWARD,
RELEASING LURE WHEN ROD IS
STOPPED OVER TARGET

FIGURE 48.

THE OVERHEAD CAST

Let's note that stopping the rod at a position of "about" twelve o'clock has been recommended. The rod should be stopped a bit sooner if it is a very light and whippy one. Otherwise, the backward sweep of the lure may be too great, causing the trajectory of flight to be too high.

Try this cast by using the forearm, with almost no bending of the wrist, and then by using the wrist only. Light, whippy rods may make the latter variation work best. A few practice casts soon will establish the ideal variation for use with any specific rod.

THE BACKHAND CAST

This is a side cast made from the left instead of from the right, as shown in Figure 49. Its primary advantage is to allow sending a lure to a reasonable distance when there are obstructions behind the angler, overhead, and to his right. As such, it may be called an emergency cast, not recommended if one of the others is possible.

To make it, the forearm is held high horizontally in front of the body, with the rod pointing downward to the left as far as the tackle and the position of the caster will permit. From this position, the angler uses his wrist to snap the rod backward slightly and then immediately outward and upward in the direction of the target, releasing the lure when the rod is stopped pointing slightly over the lure's objective.

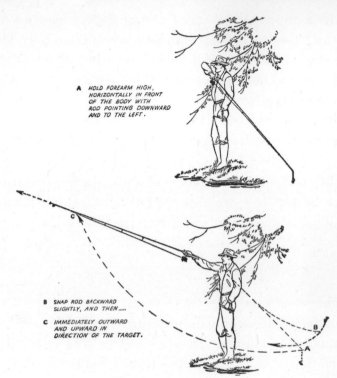

A HOLD FOREARM HIGH,
HORIZONTALLY IN FRONT
OF THE BODY WITH
ROD POINTING DOWNWARD
AND TO THE LEFT.

C

B SNAP ROD BACKWARD
SLIGHTLY, AND THEN.....

C IMMEDIATELY OUTWARD
AND UPWARD IN
DIRECTION OF THE TARGET.

FIGURE 49.

THE BACKHAND CAST

THE FLIP CAST

This one will drop a lure very accurately, but will not send it to a great distance. As such, it is useful for fishing nearby spots in small streams, or on ponds and lakes where the lure must land between obstructions such as grasses and lily pads, and where a long cast is not needed.

Many anglers like to use this cast with at least a foot of line between rod tip and lure, in order to give the lure an action somewhat resembling that of a pendulum. In this case, the cast must be made very slowly. The fisherman points his rod toward the target and slightly downward. From this position, the rod is snapped upward through a very small arc and then

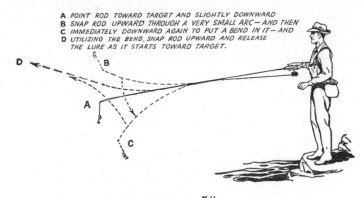

FIGURE 50.

THE FLIP CAST

immediately downward again, to put a bend in it. Utilizing this bend, the rod is snapped upward again, the lure being released as this last upward sweep directs it toward the target. The procedure for doing this is sketched in Figure 50. To gain proficiency in it, the flip cast requires a bit of practice in timing; but, once it is mastered, it is a very handy one to use. With it, the angler can poke his rod through a hole in the bushes along a stream and send his lure outward for

fifty feet or more from the most difficult of casting positions. Determining the length of line between rod tip
and lure depends upon judgment influenced by practice. Small lures used with stiff rods should be cast
with a longer line than heavier lures with rods which
are more whippy. In fact, a fairly whippy rod, such as
some of those made of glass fiber, will cast a relatively
heavy lure best when there is only a very small amount
of line between lure and rod tip. Many fishermen like
to see how far and how accurately they can direct the
lure with a minimum of flexing of the rod. A total upward and downward arc of not much over two feet
often will suffice for a good cast. A second version of
the flip cast calls for a minimum amount of line between lure and rod tip. The secret of this also is in
timing, coupled with flexing the rod with rhythmic
but very short and quick twitches of the wrist.

THE ARROW, OR CATAPULT, CAST

This works best with glass rods. When it is used
with a bamboo rod, care should be taken not to bend
the rod beyond its elastic limit. It has a practical use
in allowing a lure to be shot under branches hanging
over the water.

To make it, as shown in Figure 51, grasp the lure
carefully behind the barb of the hook, with sufficient
line between lure and rod tip so that, by pulling back
the left arm and extending the right one slightly, the
rod is made to flex in the same manner that one draws

A. *GRASP LURE BEHIND BARB OF HOOK AND PULL BACK ON LURE
TO FLEX ROD, POINTING ROD TOWARD TARGET*

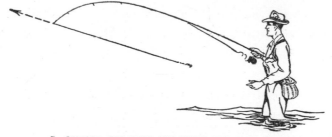

B. *RELEASE THE LURE AND THEN THE LINE, THUS MAKING
THE BEND IN THE ROD SHOOT THE LURE FORWARD.*

FIGURE 51.

THE ARROW CAST

a bow. By pointing the butt of the rod toward the target and releasing the lure held by the thumb and
forefinger of the left hand, the bent rod will make the
lure fly forward. Immediately after releasing the lure,
the angler allows the pull on the line to remove it
from the forefinger of his rod hand.

After any of these casts have been made, it is usual
practice to follow the path of the lure with the rod
tip and to hold the rod tip fairly low, approximately

pointing at the lure. This allows the line to put minimum wear upon itself and upon the guides of the rod. It also allows the angler to elevate the rod quickly in striking a fish.

ON CASTING FROM OBSTRUCTED POSITIONS

A great advantage of spinning is that it permits casting virtually from any place along stream or lake, regardless of whether or not there are bushes or rocks behind the angler, overhead, at either or both sides, or even in front of him! If one is reasonably adept at making all of the five casts described above, fishing near obstructions means very little — because one or more of the casts recommended can be made from almost any conceivable position.

ADVANTAGES OF PUMPING FISH

It is very important to stress again that, in playing a fish, the angler must not turn the handle of his reel unless he is recovering line. If he turns the reel handle against the slipping clutch, he accomplishes nothing except to put a bad twist in his line. In handling a strong fish, the rod should be raised high, to aid the brake by adding to it the drag caused by the friction of the guides on the line. When enough line has been recovered to raise the rod tip to maximum height, the angler can lower the tip and reel in line at the same time, repeating this procedure as often as necessary.

If this added drag is insufficient, the angler can give

temporary added braking power to the reel by pressure of the forefinger of the rod hand or by cradling the reel in his left hand and applying light thumb and finger pressure to the spool as shown in Picture 5 of "Casting Positions." As he does this, he raises the rod tip and then recovers line by reeling as the tip is lowered. This method of aiding the drag of the reel is called "pumping," and even very large fish can be brought in with light tackle by this means. Before starting to pump in a fish, the anti-reverse lever on the reel should be engaged to prevent the reel from backwinding when the reel hand is removed from the reel handle. As a matter of fact, I have found it a good precaution always to engage the anti-reverse immediately upon hooking a fish of respectable size.

SUGGESTION FOR PRACTICE CASTING

When one buys a new spinning outfit, the primary instinct seems to be to go out and try it on the lawn, if no water is convenient. This puts the spinning outfit under a great disadvantage. On the ground, the lure has a tendency to bump and hop along, making the line come back onto the reel spool in a series of tight and loose coils. Since it is important to reel in line under steady tension, "lawn fishing" is inclined to make the angler cast badly because he does not have the advantage of the steady drag on the lure offered when casting over water. Here, it may be well to stress again that line should be wound onto the reel spool under constant tension. Lacking this, all reels have a tendency to wind line high on the rear of the spool, often influencing it to fall forward in loose coils. These loose coils may cast off several at a time, rather than consecutively, causing several coils to be pulled from the spool at one time, thus resulting in a tangle of line at the gathering guide. Recovering line under steady tension nearly always is the solution to this easily avoidable difficulty.

If one wishes to try dry-land casting, it will help to obtain a lady's kid-glove finger and to fill it with a quarter of an ounce or so of sand, sewing up the end and attaching a snap swivel. The weighted glove finger, used instead of a lure, bounces about much less and is the best thing I know of for practice casting of this sort.

CHAPTER NINE

Fast Water Spinning

ONCE IN A WHILE I have the privilege of going fishing with an elderly gentleman who has forgotten far more about the complexities of angling than most of us ever will know. When we reach the stream, it is his custom to rig his tackle with exceeding care. Then, unlike so many who rush in to start haphazard casting, he goes up to a selected position on the bank and leisurely sits down! I have learned to sit beside him, quietly smoking and watching the river — studying its rocks, its riffles, its pockets and its currents, and deciding the probable positions of the larger fish.

"No use casting," he once said, "until you decide where the fish are, where to stand to cast for them, and how to plan the casts. Saves time and trouble to figure it out in the first place!"

After many minutes of silent observation, the old angler will roam to a planned position and will cast to a selected spot. As likely as not, he will take a good fish on the first cast. He plans his strategy like the veteran that he is. He does more sitting than any man I know; he does far less casting — and he invariably catches more fish!

NOTES ON FINDING FISH IN STREAMS

Taking a big one occasionally may be an accident. Taking big ones consistently is the reward of skill and understanding. Part of the understanding is to realize that fish are more like people than people might think. They seek waters of certain temperatures, and they shun abodes that are too hot or too cold, just as people do. They have a rather human characteristic of not wanting to travel farther than necessary for their food, and of having shade and sanctuary within reach in times of alarm. When conditions are right, they will feed to the bursting point. When it is too sunny, too hot, or too cold, they may be relatively dormant and eat scarcely at all.

While the various species of trout choose slightly different feeding and resting positions in a stream,[1] in general, they are basically the same. They all like the relatively quiet water in front of or behind large rocks in a current because the rocks act as obstructions to the flow, guiding the fast current to the sides or above, and leaving slow water upstream and downstream of them. The rocks, as shown in Figure 52, offer good resting and feeding positions, with places of concealment and protection as well. Trout also like to feed in the slow water of the slope below a riffle, as shown in Figure 53, but usually will not be

[1] As described in detail in my book *Trout Waters and How to Fish Them*.

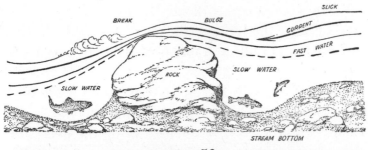

FIGURE 52.

"HOLDING POSITIONS" FOR FISH IN THE SLOW
WATER ABOVE AND BEHIND A ROCK

there unless actively feeding, since such places, if relatively shallow, will provide insufficient concealment.
They are found in the slow water which is near to the
faster current, where they can rest and wait for the
current to bring food to them. In such waters, look for
them most often near places where they can find protection.

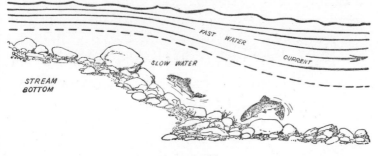

FIGURE 53.

"FEEDING POSITIONS" FOR FISH IN THE SLOW
WATER OF A STREAM

When streams are in flood, the fish usually will lie deep because the force of the current near the bottom of a stream is only a fraction of what it is near the surface.

The reasons why fish behave as they do are complex. Their study brings great rewards to the angler. Their requisites may be summed up in the necessities of food, comfort and concealment.

Thus, if we wish to adopt the habit of the old angler, a few minutes devoted to the study of a stream will indicate where the force of the current is taking the food, where the current is broken to provide resting places, and where there are rocks, undercut banks, deep holes and shading trees and bushes to offer concealment. In any stream, such ideal positions comprise relatively small areas of the water's surface. These are what the old angler was observing. Usually, it pays to concentrate upon them, to the exclusion of haphazard casting.

HOW TO FISH A TYPICAL STREAM

Some of the more probable productive locations in a stream are indicated in the sketch in Figure 54. Let's fish down through this spot and see what happens!

The angler standing at X should make casts 2 and 3 from farther upstream, or perhaps from farther downstream in the manner of casts 9 and 10 from posi-

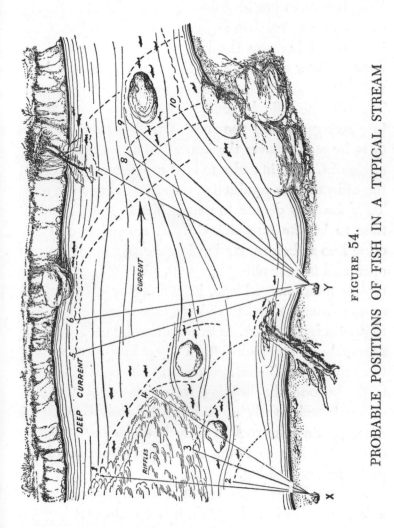

FIGURE 54.

PROBABLE POSITIONS OF FISH IN A TYPICAL STREAM

tion Y. We must assume that, when trying them from X, he is too close to his fish — but since he is in this location he may try it in any case. His cast to Position 1 is excellent because the lure will swing through the deeper water at the tail of the riffle, which we have noted is a good feeding position for trout. To make his lure skirt the riffle, he must recover line slightly as the lure swings toward the rock. The first time he casts thus, he may recover the lure when it has reached the angle of Cast 4, in order to continue fishing the tail of the riffle and the productive water just above the rock. Then, he may decide to make Cast 1 again, and this time to let the lure sink deeper, rather than recovering line as before. He has left the pickup of his reel open and is controlling line with his forefinger. If the rock is a submerged one, he will allow some line to escape from the reel to sink his lure more deeply and to drift it by the rock. In this manner he can cover the near side of the rock with a deep lure after having worked the holding water back of the rock. Cast 4 is made beyond the holding water ahead of the rock and is fished deeply as close to the rock as possible. After passing the rock, a little line can be let out to enable the lure to swing to the position around the partly submerged log.

In making Cast 4, and in other casts to the presumable positions of feeding fish, it is well to cast beyond the spot and to recover the lure through it, or to cast slightly upstream and allow the lure to swing into the feeding position. If the lure should be dropped on the position itself, the probable result would be to frighten the fish. In such casting, it also is well to brake and then to stop the lure just over the spot where we want it to land, so that it will meet the water quietly, rather than falling into it with a splash.

Now, let's walk downstream to Position Y. We will try Casts 5 and 6 from here, rather than from X, because the far bank is steep, indicating that the water is deep. A cast slightly upstream with a little slack in the line will allow the lure to sink more readily into the slower water beneath the surface and the current will make it drift to the holding positions near the rock. If the water here is very deep, we may need to let a little line out to make the lure travel even deeper. This can be controlled so accurately with the forefinger that the lure will work with the current and yet we can feel a strike instantly on the relatively tight line and just as instantly snub the outflow of the line and hook the fish.

Cast 6 is made to the far bank to a spot which Cast 5 already has covered. The lure is guided as closely as possible to the rock and then is allowed to swing across the stream to cover the holding water above the rock farther downstream. It can be fished in along the rocks on the near shore. Since the main current is on the far side of the stream, the near shore current may be too slow to hold many fish, but it may as well be tried.

A tree has been uprooted from the top of the far bank and has slid down, with some of its branches submerged. Trees such as this shelter insects which periodically drop into the water. They furnish sanctuary of a sort to small food fish, and they offer protection and shade to game fish. Therefore, we cast as near to the branches as possible, remembering that an overcast can hang us up badly. On one of these casts, the lure is allowed to drift downstream and to work as nearly behind the tree as is possible. Cast 8 is made upstream of the large rock and beyond it, so that its swing will cover the holding water just upstream of the rock. Cast 9 is sent a bit farther out and closer to the rock, and the lure is made to work as near to it as possible. If the rock happens to be below water, the lure can be allowed to drift deeper downstream to cover the back of the rock as well. If not, the back can be covered from farther downstream. Lastly, Cast 10 takes care of the inshore side of the rock. It can be made upstream and allowed to drift downstream, or it can be made downstream and worked up through the holding water on the downstream side.

While fishing this stretch, it is important to gauge the depth of the travel of the lure and to be sure that it sinks into the slow current deep in the river. Many fish will not rise up through the fast water to take a lure, even if they can see it. The lure must be worked down to them. We have noted that there are relatively heavy lures which sink quickly and which are valuable in deep, fast currents; also relatively light lures which will ride even a slow current safely in shallow water. The choice between them is important. I have fished fast streams where anglers who did not get their lures deep enough caught no fish. Those who fished them deeply enjoyed strike after strike.

This brings up the question of upstream fishing; a method which I am convinced frequently takes large fish when nothing else will work. It is well to select a lure which needs no extra weight, rather than a light one above which lead must be added. A compact wobbling spoon often is just the ticket.

In upstream fishing, the idea is to keep the lure moving downstream just a little bit faster than the current. When a fish swims downstream, he must move faster than the current in order to breathe with his gills properly. Thus, correct speed in fishing the lure gives it action more nearly like the bait fish it is intended to represent.

If we can estimate the speed of the current and keep the lure moving a bit faster, the lure will operate very close to the bottom, and there will be less danger of its getting hooked up. In fast streams, big fish usually lie close to the bottom, and upstream fishing is an excellent way to take them.

Fishing properly, the angler can feel his lure bump bottom occasionally. If it does not, he probably is retrieving it too fast. Let it bump — even at the expense of getting caught up once in a while. It may cost a few lures, but it will get more fish! Spinning is an excellent way to fish upstream because the fast retrieve of the reel (twenty-five inches or so with every turn of the handle) can pull a lure downstream much faster than the swiftest current can carry it. Select the lure's path of travel carefully to bring it as closely as possible to the feeding and resting positions we have described. And, don't forget to try this method from the tail of a large pool, fan-casting the entire fishable part with enough casts to cover the bottom thoroughly. Big fish do not like to chase lures very far. They may feel that the small bit of supposed food hardly is worth the effort.

Getting "hung up" on the stream bottom is a not-always-avoidable nuisance. The beginner is inclined to lose his patience and to jerk at the lure, thus imbedding it more securely. The experienced spinning fisherman tries to decide how his lure is caught. Usually, he can free it easily by pulling in the opposite direction from that in which the lure was traveling when it became snagged.

If one is caught up beyond hope of release, the only alternative is to break. Reel in as much line as possible, with the rod pointing at the lure, so as not to strain it. Hold the reel spool from turning and back away slowly until the line exceeds the limit of its strength, causing something to give way. A steady pull often will free the lure, and the tackle will be regained intact. Nine out of ten snagged lures can be recovered by using intelligence, but as many will be lost by impatient tactics.

STREAM FISHING IN MAINE

Let's see how some of the situations we have discussed will work on an actual fishing trip — in this case, to the wilderness of northwestern Maine.

Dana McNally, operator of McNally's Sporting Camps, meets us at his seaplane dock at the little town of Portage and flies us to his comfortable cabins on his island at Fish Lake, which is our base of operations.

"Just finished building a new camp at Sebamticook," he reports. "There are some big trout in the lake and also in the stream. Why not go in there for a few days?"

Sebamticook is as far into the Maine woods as one can get without starting to come out to semicivilization on the Canadian side. The unspoiled lakes, streams and forests have been left relatively undisturbed to the bear, the deer, the moose, the birds and — to the fish.

I pricked up my ears at Dana's mention of "some big trout" because I have come to learn that "trout" to him mean only Eastern brook trout, and that "big" ones indicate fish of trophy size. The others casually are disregarded as being too commonplace to mention.

We completed the half-hour flight to Sebamticook

just before dark and settled ourselves in the warmth of the little cabin, perched on a bluff where the stream joins the lake.

"There's an old buster of a trout up the stream aways," Dana remarked, as we headed up river in the canoe after breakfast. "Can't seem to take him on a fly. Maybe you can do it by spinning."

The place was a deep, fast run on a bend of the stream. A great tree had fallen into the water; its protecting branches splaying into the dark depths wherein the trout was supposed to dwell. I fished the place industriously for an hour or more and took a few one and two pounders from it, but the big fish was not in evidence. Later, I returned and tried it again.

I should have realized that the run was five or six feet deep, and so swift that my lures were not getting down near the bottom. If the trout was there, he must be lying deep and refusing to rise for the lure. It reminded me of the turbulent rivers of the Pacific northwest, where the steelhead and salmon often do the same thing. "Bump the bottom" and "get down to the fish" are the maxims of the anglers who get the big ones.

Accordingly, I selected a small but relatively heavy copper wobbler and cast it to the far bank twenty-five feet or so upstream from the fallen tree. With the pickup of the reel open, I released a few coils of line to let the lure go deep. When it hit bottom, the signal telegraphed itself to the rod, and an occasional twitch of the tip kept it in motion. I tried to figure its path as it shimmered and bounced over the stones of the river bed, and I hoped that there were no submerged sticks or crevices to hang it up as it traveled along.

When it seemed to have reached the tree, its motion stopped. After getting it where I had wanted it to go, it must have become snagged on a branch of the tree, I thought — but I gave it an exploratory twitch with the rod tip in any case.

Whatever was holding it in the black depths struck back. I was fast to a trout, and evidently a big one. To keep him from winding the four-pound monofilament around the branches, I leaned back on the rod as much as I dared — and succeeded in turning him into the middle of the stream. This done, it was possible to hold him there while I waded downstream to get him above me. In this position, he had to fight the current, and the rod as well.

He was a rather disappointing fighter, as so many really big fish are. After a few rushes here and there, he drifted down to me and I lifted him from the water by grasping him over the back with thumb and forefinger behind his gill covers.

The trout proved to be a hook-jawed old male, twenty-six inches long. In his prime, he must have weighed in the vicinity of eight pounds, but he now was as thin as a pike and by my pocket scales he weighed only four pounds and a half. Dana took a picture of him and I let him go, holding him upright in the water until he had regained enough strength to swim away. The old man of the river slowly wavered back to his sanctuary among the submerged branches, and I hope he was able to live out his few remaining months in peace.

Farther upstream we came to a shelving riffle. A cast over the shelf allowed the little wobbler to ride toward me on a tight line until I gave it enough slack to make it slide over the shelf into the depths below the riffle. Several trout were feeding under the shelf. Most of them were half-pounders, and they slashed at the little lure as savagely as wild little trout are inclined to do. As I was playing with one of them, a mink tried to cross the stream near the riffle. The current was too strong for him and he was forced to quarter toward me, swimming frantically as the water bore him toward my rod tip. At one point I could have reached out and touched him, but he slowly made progress, suspiciously watching me the while with his beady black eyes, and finally scurried up the bank of the opposite shore.

At high noon, a slight breeze wafted down-river the faint odor of bacon and coffee, mingled with the fragrant scents of balsam and the dampness of the woods. Around the bend, Dana was waiting beside a small fire he had built among the rocks. Coffee bubbled in his battered and blackened pot, and four pink trout fillets curled and sputtered amid bacon in the pan.

While we had lunch, Dana pointed to a log stuck in the bank and jutting out into the stream.

"Went down to the spring for some water," he said. "Just as I stepped on the log I saw a big trout lying downstream of it. He saw me, but that was half an hour ago. . . . Really a big one," he added significantly.

From a distance, the water below the log seemed about two feet deep, and evidently the bank was undercut, with the bare roots of trees extending into the stream. We discussed the situation and decided to try for him from upstream with a spinner. I put on a copper-bladed C. P. Swing in one of the larger sizes and cast it downstream to a place slightly above the log, where its blade, held in place by the current, twirled merrily a few inches under the surface. Letting out a few coils of line allowed it to sink and drift below the log, where I left it alone, except for an occasional twitch of the rod tip. There, the little spinner covered a square yard or so of water where the big trout was supposed to be. But nothing happened.

After a few minutes of waiting, without moving the lure, I glanced at Dana, who was comfortably sitting on the bank watching my efforts with a questioning look in his eyes.

"He won't take it," I needlessly remarked, "and I don't dare cast over him too much. I'll just leave the spinner where it is for ten minutes or so. Maybe he'll get annoyed enough to hit it."

I could see the occasional glint of the spinner under the shadow of the log and knew it was where Dana had said the fish was lying. Eight minutes had gone by and nothing had happened. But suddenly the water swirled and I was fast to the fish.

Under the prick of the barb, he tore out into the stream. His weight and the current prevented me from gaining on him. When he struck, I instinctively had engaged the anti-reverse lever of the reel, and now I cupped my left hand under the reel so that my thumb and fingers could provide an added brake to keep the clutch from slipping. I could not get below the fish but, by the pumping method, I succeeded in the much less desirable expedient of working him upstream toward me. I led him into the shallow water of an eddy and beached him. He weighed exactly six pounds.

"Never saw that done before," Dana said. "How did you know he would hit after all that time?"

"I didn't," I admitted, "but I was trying a theory that has paid off occasionally before."

WHY FISH TAKE LURES

And then, with the big trout laid out on ferns between us, I told him what my old friend, Herbie Welch, had told me many years ago.

"Trout don't always strike because they are hungry," this grand old angler had said. "They also take lures for three other reasons: because they are made angry, because they become curious, or they may take them in the spirit of play."

I never have forgotten Herb Welch's remark, and it behooves me to pass it on to others, because it is a tried and true fact that, if fish won't take lures because of hunger, they often can be made to take them by these other means.

In this case, the idea was to make the big trout angry. He had a favorite resting place, and he wanted it all to himself. He had no interest in the lure as food, but when it so constantly hovered near him, he finally became annoyed at the whirling flash of its blade and he struck at it to kill it and get it out of the way.

I have discussed in *Trout Waters and How to Fish Them* the applications of these four reasons why fish take lures, and so shall not go into details here except to add that many of the garish flies and peculiar lures that take fish occasionally probably do so because the fish are playful, angry or curious, rather than because they are hungry. The hunger theory, calling for fairly exact imitation of their foods in appearance and action, usually is the best one to start with. But if it brings no results, it may be well to change tactics and to try one of the other three.

WALLEYED PIKE IN CANADA

Occasionally I go to the famous Sassamaskin-Vassal Fish and Game Reserve, whose base camp is Au Rabasca Lodge, at Rivière aux Rats, just below the town of La Tuque in Quebec province. The lakes of the reserve are noted for big brook trout but, after a few days of fishing for them, I enjoy the ten-mile trip up the old tote road along Rat River to a place where there are some large walleyed pike. Here, a wide spot in the small stream gives it the appearance of a pond. I fished it for half a day once before finding out where the fish were — which proved to be below the fast water of the inlet, where the current distributes itself in the "lake."

Knowing that game fish of many types often frequent stream mouths, especially during warm water periods, I had fished the stream mouth several times and decided that the pike must be somewhere else. When I couldn't find them elsewhere, I tried the stream mouth again, anchoring the canoe a long cast downward from the inlet. Cast after cast brought no results near the surface, so I tried letting the little wobbler sink enough to bump the bottom. This tactic brought strike after strike, and a landed fish at almost every cast. The bottom of the inlet seemed to be paved with large walleyes, but I would have gone fishless if I had not tried deeply sinking the lure.

SUGGESTIONS ON BROOK FISHING

This raises a point well worth remembering when fishing stream mouths; especially in warm weather, when fish seek the cooler waters of such places and the food there which the stream brings down to them. The visible part of the stream mouth may be shallow, and probably will contain few fish. But below the visible part is a shelf or deep channel where the submerged currents of the stream mix with those of the lake. Below the shelf or in the channel usually is where the fish will be found. If we are angling from a boat, it is well to keep a good distance from the inlet because, if we pass too close to it, the chances are good that we will be over the fish and can not cast to them properly. Secondly, if surface fishing brings no results, we may hit the jackpot by working our lures deeper. Fish often will not travel very far to take a lure, even if the waters are clear enough for them to see it. A few feet usually makes a great deal of difference. We can select the proper lure and the proper place to fish it, but if it is not presented correctly to the fish, the effort may result in failure rather than in success.

In fishing from the shore, we often encounter a shelf such as this, or a transverse ledge or deep hole in the stream. On a tight line, the current will sweep the lure over the place so that it will not get to the fish which are lying deep beneath; their noses close to the step. Just before the lure reaches the drop-off, release a few coils of line from the reel to allow the lure to sink down into the hole before it passes by. This tactic, often used in fishing for steelhead and Pacific salmon, brings results when trout, bass and other game fish are found in such places.

Many fishermen have told me that they have difficulty in fishing small streams and brooks with spinning tackle because the water is so shallow that their lures catch on bottom and because they find accurate casting over short distances very difficult. Others agree that spinning tackle is better for this kind of fishing than gear of any other sort. They catch more fish with it and they have less trouble. What are the secrets of success for this kind of fishing?

Those who fish small streams habitually find light tackle very advantageous; a medium to soft rod with a pulling power of half a pound or a pound (which would be rod-size A or B in Figure 46, page 176, and would be five and a half or six feet long) coupled with a monofilament line between a pound and a half and three pounds in strength, and lures weighing between a sixteenth and an eighth of an ounce (somewhat lighter than normal for this tackle, because of no necessity for long casts and the fact that tiny lures are more efficient than larger ones for this purpose). These ultra-small lures hang better in currents, sink less readily, and make less disturbance than larger ones. For the purpose, I find spinners superior to wobblers, although a tiny wobbler or two should be tried occasionally. Such lures are less prevalent in stores than the bigger and heavier ones, but are easy to make,

Lady Anglers Can Become Very Proficient
(As shown by Mrs. Don C. Harger, of Salem, Oregon, who
took this thirty-three-pound Chinook salmon on spinning tackle)

Wide Rivers and Fast Water Offer but Mild Challenge to the Spinning Angler who Can Cast to Difficult Locations Far Across the Stream

as we have described. Little wobblers can be fashioned from spinner blades, since extra weight is not necessary for short casts.

I have already gone into detail about the importance of forefinger control; it is a very valuable advantage in this kind of fishing. Just before the little lure lands, the forefinger should stop the line and the rod tip immediately should be raised to put the lure in motion on the instant it touches the water. When the rod tip is raised, the lure can be put under control of the reel if desirable. This is the secret of preventing the lure from catching on the bottom, and extremely shallow water can be fished successfully by this method.

Since there normally is no necessity for long casts, and since often trees and bushes are in the way, the Backhand Cast, the Flip Cast, or the Arrow Cast (described in Chapter Eight) usually are better than the Side or the Overhead Casts.

My favorite lure for such fishing at the time of writing this is the well known C. P. Swing, in the one-tenth-ounce size. By the above method, it can be put in motion the instant it lands, and it will hang in a current only a few inches deep without sinking or catching on bottom. By pointing the rod toward undercut banks, rocks and other supposedly productive spots, the little spinner can be steered up- or downstream into all the nooks and corners which should hold fish.

One day, my old friend Lewis Powers and I were exploring the vast stretches of Massachusetts's Quabbin Reservoir in his outboard-motored boat. We found an inlet where there were small white perch in abundance, and we took dozens of them with the type of tackle I have just described. They wouldn't touch the larger lures, and seemed disinterested in spinners, but tiny, dull-colored wobblers fascinated them. A cast soon would attract a large school, which would follow the baby wobbler almost to the boat. Finally, when we jiggled the lure a bit, one of the larger perch would take it. On tiny tackle such as this, these miniature fish can be a great deal of fun. And their skinned fillets, dusted with bread crumbs and deep-fried to a golden brown, are a dish for the gods.

A brook entering the head of this inlet invited exploration. Lew made a cast to its mouth and promptly took a half-pound brook trout. When we found no more fish in evidence there, we wet waded and peered up its narrow alder-lined stretch. The water was so shallow that stones showed above the surface; but, in the shadow of some of the larger ones, we spied three good-sized trout. Lew made a cast above the first one. The little lure slithered downstream around the rocks in the shallow water but, with rod tip held high, he guided it near the fish, which swirled and took it as it passed by.

The next trout seemed undisturbed, and I made a cast up the brook to him. The little lure landed several

feet above him and started its shallow course downstream. The monofilament line was within a few inches
of the fish, but he seemed to ignore it, indicating
anew one of the values of this type of line for fishing. The lure had to be retrieved swiftly to keep it
from hanging up on the stones, but the trout flashed
and took it as soon as it came in sight.

The next cast to the trout farthest away went a foot
or two to the right, causing the lure to drop over an
alder branch almost above the trout. Frequently a
lure can be released from such a predicament by a
very simple expedient. When the lure stopped its
pendulum-like motion, Lew cautiously reeled in line
until the lure almost touched the branch. Then, with a
slight upward twitch of his rod, he flipped it over and
off the branch, dropping it lightly into the stream. The
trout, evidently thinking it was a bit of food falling
from the alders, grabbed it quickly. Thus, with the
help of Lady Luck, we added all four trout to our
collection of white perch and ended a very successful day.

FLY-LINE SHOOTING HEADS

Before completing this chapter, I should like to
comment on a type of fly line that has been offered to
adapt spinning tackle to fly-fishing. This consists of a
shooting head of plastic-finished fly line much heavier and shorter than that used in fly-fishing. The line
usually varies between thirty feet and ten feet in

length (the average being about fourteen feet) and
ordinarily is tapered from Size G to Size A. It can be
tied to the monofilament spinning line with a Clinch
Knot, having a loop spliced to it for this purpose. The
forward end, of course, is fitted with a leader and a
fly.

This fly-line shooting head necessarily must have
good floating characteristics, which primarily are provided by the plastic coating. It is reeled in until the
joining loop is a few inches from the rod tip and is cast
as a fly line is cast, but with the pickup of the reel
open (and the line controlled by the forefinger) to allow use of the spinning line as a shooting line.

It takes a bit of practice to lay the line out and to
turn the tip over as neatly as one can with a fly rod,
but, with a fairly long spinning rod, it can be mastered without undue difficulty. False casts and power
casts (the double line-hand haul) are made as with
a fly rod, except for variations in the timing. Because
of their added wind-resistance, bass bugs and
streamer flies seem to lay out better than do small wet
or dry flies, but most anglers will find that they can
use all varieties adequately well.

My observations have been that, with this acces-
sory, the average angler can cast about fifty or sixty
feet of line, but not much more. This, of course, is
enough under ordinary circumstances. The rig cannot take the place of a fly rod, and it is not intended
to. I think that many spinning fishermen will enjoy

trying it and, with this shooting line to provide the casting weight needed in spinning, plus a box of flies and a leader or two in one's jacket, it is quite obvious that we have a useful fly-fishing appliance to increase the already wide latitude of usefulness of our spinning tackle.

CHAPTER TEN

Spinning on Ponds and Lakes

WHEN EXPERIENCED ANGLERS observe the boats on a lake, the conclusion invariably drawn is that most of them are indulging in rather aimless fishing. The majority come to dock with whatever Lady Luck and coincidence combine to provide. A relative few, however, return with impressive catches and the fishermen in them modestly may admit that they released a good many more. Innocent bystanders dismiss these extremes of fortune as being purely the "luck" of angling, but everybody keeps a weather eye out to see just where the fortunate boats go the next day!

These dockside post-mortems remind me of the ancient story about the half-wit who found the lost horse which no one else had been able to locate. While searchers fruitlessly roamed the countryside, the half-wit managed to figure out where he would like to go if he were a horse. He went there, and there it was!

Fishing in ponds and lakes is somewhat the same, in that experienced anglers need do no more than a minimum of fruitless searching. They know that each variety of fish seeks its own definite types of places in which to live and to feed; that these areas make fishing in all the rest of the lake unnecessary, and that favored locations gradually may change with altering seasonal conditions. They know how to interpret these conditions, and thus to decide where the fish will be.

To throw a little light on this subject, let's combine some of the features of a pond and of a lake into the sketch in Figure 55 and assume that the more important species of lake and pond fish are resident there. First, we'll take a boat and go fishing for trout.

Where lakes freeze over in winter, the big trout remain in deep water until spring. When surface waters warm up a bit, many of them will go to the rocky shallows to feed. We note that the island has a shelving, rocky shore line and that a gravel bar extends from the point of land to the island, so we cover these spots thoroughly in the spring. We also fish along the wooded shore line from the stream inlet to the brook because the rocky, shelving bottom, protected by foliage along the shore, also offers a combination of warmer surface waters, protection and food.

As spring advances, surface waters in these areas may grow too warm for trout, since most of the species prefer temperatures ranging from 50° to 70° Fahrenheit. They will leave the vicinity of the gravel bar and of the island, but a few still will frequent the deeper wooded shore line, especially where cool runoff water from the hills seeps into the lake as springs. The cove is deep, well shaded, and filled with stumps

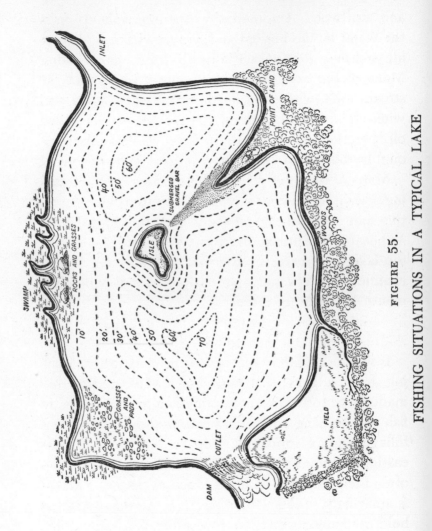

FIGURE 55.

FISHING SITUATIONS IN A TYPICAL LAKE

and driftwood. Undoubtedly, springs well up from the water on the bottom and, if so, trout may be here all summer long, especially in northern climates. Many of the trout will take up positions around the stream inlet, where the incoming water is cooler and where food is washed down to them. A boat anchored off the inlet allows the angler to cover the area thoroughly, both near the surface and deeper down.

Many of the trout will inhabit the brook mouth during warm weather, for the same reasons. In fishing this spot, we take care to keep the boat well off shore — because the brook has carved a channel out into the lake, and many of the trout will be lying in this channel, rather than in the visible part of the brook mouth between its shores.

TROLLING WITH SPINNING TACKLE

It will be best to cover most of these places by casting from a slowly moving boat. Casts should be made as close to the shore as possible because many fish will be lying under the protection of overhanging foliage and of logs and rocks in the water. While casting covers a greater area, trolling the shore line often is equally or even more effective. Spinning tackle is amazingly suitable for trolling. If we don't wish to hold the spinning rod, we can put it in a rod holder, engaging the anti-reverse lock and setting the brake so that it will give line under a pull only slightly stronger than that caused by the speed of the boat.

By this means, an angler can fish effectively and can control his craft at the same time. When a fish strikes, the light drag of the reel will hook him, but will not pull the hook from his mouth. There usually is plenty of time to stop the boat and to pick up the rod while the fish is taking line from the reel on his initial run.

Three fishermen can troll very comfortably from a small boat, as Figure 56 suggests. Note that the outboard rods have at least fifty feet of line out, but that

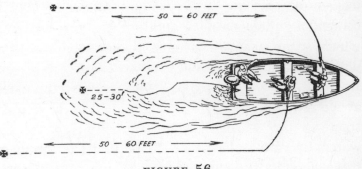

FIGURE 56.

POSITIONS OF RODS IN TROLLING

the inboard rod trolls its lure just beyond the propeller wash. Fish come up to investigate the disturbance caused by the propeller. If the inboard lure does not hook them, one of the outboard lures may, as they pass by. The boat is traveling at a speed of about five miles per hour — or a bit faster than a man can walk. This relatively fast speed usually attracts more fish when trolling Bead-Bucks and other long streamer flies, baits or spinners. Wobbling spoons should be trolled a little slower, to keep them from revolving and to give them proper action. When trolling streamer flies and other nontwisting lures, keels and swivels are not necessary but, if the lure has even the slightest tendency to revolve, the use of a keel and one or two swivels are most important.

In summer trolling for cold water fish, such as big trout (especially "togue" or "Mackinaw trout," "Kamloops" rainbows and "Dolly Vardens") and landlocked salmon, the troller should follow a definite route along the contour of depth of the "thermocline," which is the deep intermediary layer separating the warm surface water from the cold depths of a lake. In *Trout Waters and How to Fish Them*, I discussed at considerable length the importance of understanding the seasonal temperature changes of the waters at various levels in a lake and the influence these changes have upon the depths where cold water fish are to be found. Anglers who have adopted this simple rule of locating proper fishing depths have learned that it makes all the difference in the world between finding fish and not finding them in summer. These cold water fish feed near the surface in the cold water of early spring and late fall, but they remain at a definite and determinable level during the warm surface water period in summer. Since they then are bottom feeders and must frequent the shore line at this depth, it follows that the "path of good trolling" is along the appropriate contour and at its level (such as the thirty-foot contour sketched in Figure 55). If lures are trolled at this depth on this path (as indicated by contour maps), one should find in this relatively small area the greatest concentration of fish.

Landlocked salmon and togue like water which is even colder than temperatures suited to most of the trouts and charrs. They come to the surface in early spring and late fall, returning to the thermocline level in summer. Landlocked salmon near the surface feed in the gravelly shallows and habitually follow schools of smelt, which travel slowly along the shore to streams for spawning and thus can be located from day to day during their migratory run. Both togue (lake trout) and landlocked salmon frequent stream mouths during cold water periods.

If the lake contains smallmouthed bass, they will be found in moderately cold or cool water where there is shade, food and protection. A shaded shore line containing large rocks is an excellent abode for bass. When they can be taken on the surface, a popping plug is one of my favorites, particularly if it can be cast into watery holes between rocks, or so close to the shore line that it appears to have dropped from the bushes. When surface waters are warmer and bass lie deeper, a small floating-diving plug, a deep running plug, or a wobbling spoon with a bucktail fly attached should be good choices — and let's not forget the plastic ball float used with bait, as described earlier!

In Figure 55, we should find bass in the grass and lily-pad area on the shallow side of the lake, because the vegetation in the water offers the shade, food and protection which they require. Since this is an ideal place for frogs, a surface lure which resembles one may be appropriate. Cast it directly to the lily pads to make it act as if it had jumped off, and fish it in the manner in which a live frog would swim if he were trying to escape from a lurking bass. In covering this area, it is well to fish the lake side of the pads before going farther into the cove. This way, fan casting to nearby spots will not disturb the fish nearer shore, and they can be covered later.

If this shallow, lily-pad area is not productive during the day, let's leave it alone and come back to it when the sun sets. The bass may be in deeper, cooler water and, if so, undoubtedly will move into these shallows soon after dusk to feed. Evening fishing in such places is more resultful in the summer when the shallow water is too warm during the day. But the pad and grass area is a storehouse of food, and bass should feed there from early evening until late into the night. If we return quietly about dark we almost surely will hear them splashing and feeding. A weed guard over the hook of a popping plug will keep it from snagging, and a relatively strong line of from four to six pounds test will help if the bass decides to tangle himself around the stems of the pads.

Although areas such as these are favorite ones for

bass, it is not generally realized that they are found just as frequently in offshore shoal water around submerged weed beds, particularly where there are large rocks and expanses of gravel harboring their food. Bass are carnivorous; they are very fond of crayfish, helgrammites and other insect larvae, fresh water shrimps, salamanders, frogs, mice, tiny turtles and many other things, including any baitfish they can swallow.

Shallow areas with lily pads and grass also are good locations for pickerel. They do not object to warm water and can be caught in summer even during the heat of the day. Most of them will be within a few feet of the shore, hidden in the grasses and under the pads. They are not a bit fussy in their choice of lures and usually will rush from their hiding places to strike at anything small that moves. If they won't take a spinner or a wobbler, either they aren't there or they can't be very hungry! Frequently it helps to remove the bare hook of a wobbler and to replace it with a dressed hook; perhaps of red and white or yellow and white hair or feathers. The sharp teeth of the pickerel have a bad habit of biting off spinning lures unless a short, fine wire leader is used. (The way to make one has been described in Chapter Five.)

HOW TO TAKE SMALLER FISH

Even though the larger pond and lake fish are sought most frequently, we can enjoy great fun with the smaller ones, such as perch, bream, crappie and bluegills. Spinning for them is excellent sport with the lighter outfits which will cast the tiniest of plugs, wobbling spoons, spinners or baits in weights of one-eighth ounce or less. Many of these fish have very small mouths and can take nothing but the very smallest of lures. Among my favorites are small wet flies which, with this light tackle, can be cast more than far enough by adding a split shot or two to the line. These colorful little fish are not timid and can be seen on the pebbly bottom near docks, among lily pads, or along the shore line. Despite their diminutive sizes, many of them are surprisingly good fighters when caught with tiny tackle, or with miniature outfits.

I am convinced that all anglers who like pond or brook fishing should own a miniature spinning outfit for small game fish. My favorite is an Alcedo Micron reel and a five-foot split-bamboo rod so delicate that I have to use fly-rod snake guides for all but the gathering guide, because the conventional spinning rod guides are so heavy they impair the rod's action. Rods such as this usually must be made to order, but I think they can be purchased from C. F. Orvis and Company, of Manchester, Vermont, or from Traver Tackle, Inc., of North Syracuse, New York. Lines should be of monofilament, testing two pounds or less. In addition to the miniature lures we have described, Heddon, South Bend and other manufacturers make fly-rod-sized lures and tiny plugs which cast very well with this tackle. Long casts are not necessary and, for these little fish, the miniature outfit does quite well enough. It brings small pond fish into the realm of sport and is a most valuable addition to the fun of spinning.

The French sport of taking larger fish on tackle of this sort — *ultra-léger* or extremely light casting — works on the proven theory that only the lightest tension need be put on a fish. The prick of the hook and the influence of the line will keep him moving. If he can be kept moving (and away from obstructions) he will become exhausted and can be brought to net. As I have said, the goal of *ultra-léger* is to take fish weighing at least ten times the strength of the line. This means, for example, taking a ten-pound fish on a line testing only a pound, or a fifty-pound fish on a line testing not more than five pounds! The goal is a hard one to reach, and perhaps impossible with some species. The practice has been criticized by a few very eminent anglers because fish are so liable to break off and so be forced to wander about with lures in their mouths until the farsightedness of nature helps them to get rid of them. This objection seems debatable. At any rate *ultra-léger* is the very opposite of the more common practice of using tackle so strong that the fish never have a fair chance. I never have valued a fish taken on tackle which gave him less than an even opportunity for gaining freedom. Hauling in fish on gear too strong for them seems to me to be "meat fishing" rather than "sport fishing." If we give our fish more than an even break, the fun, the sportsmanship, the suspense and the pride of accomplishment seems more than worth the risk involved.

"ANGLE OF APPROACH" OF LURES

On a warm and sunny day in June, a friend enticed me to a lake purported to harbor some very large bass. We circled the shore line in a boat, casting to every nook and cranny and to every hole in the lily pads farther out but, as far as results were concerned, we might as well have been fishing in a bathtub at home.

An hour of this proved that the surface water was too warm for bass and that popping plugs and similar top-water lures would be unproductive until nearer evening.

A point of land extending to an island indicated a gravel bar or ledge between the two. We decided to anchor near it to fish the shelving bottom extending out from the ten-foot depth which we dimly could see beneath us. By casting outward and allowing the lures to sink, we made their paths of travel conform to the contour of the bottom as it rose from the depths to the gravel bar near the boat. By this means we took several bass but, despite the fact that we both were fishing the same water with the same kind of lure, one of us took a noticeably larger number of fish than did the other.

The only difference we could observe in our methods was that the luckier fisherman retrieved with his rod tip held down close to the water's surface, while the less lucky one retrieved with his rod held high. We reversed the two methods and, when we did so, the degree of our success reversed. In an effort to learn the meaning of this, I later described it to an old friend who is very experienced in spinning. His comments are included in the following paragraph.

When one is standing in a boat, with his rod held high, the tip of the rod may be ten feet or more above the water. Retrieving a lure under such circumstances evidently causes it to act less enticingly and more unnaturally than when the lure's angle of approach is lessened by keeping the rod tip held low. In recent years, it has become my habit ordinarily to fish with the rod held low; even to manipulating the tip only a few inches above the water. In addition to this decreased angle of approach of the lure, it seems easier to strike and to control a fish by this means because one can strike upward or to the side with less line to contend with. After the fish has been hooked, of course the rod should be held high in the normal manner to obtain greatest use of its resiliency. I have experimented with both methods in fishing fast water from a boat and afoot from high banks and it seems to me that holding the rod low is much easier and more productive than is the practice of many fishermen in holding it high.

NIGHT FISHING

After supper on the day of our bass excursion, we decided to try night fishing in the shallows along the shore line. It was so cloudy that the weeds and pads of the shallow water were difficult to distinguish, and we had to do our fishing more by touch than by sight. As we drifted into a backwater, a resounding splash disturbed the quiet of the night and we could make out the faint shimmering "V" of his wake as the bass left for deeper water.

"That's the end of a careless frog," my companion murmured. "Try a cast or two. There must be more of them in here now."

A dense bank of clouds concealed the tiny crescent moon and, in the darkness, I reeled in my lure until it touched the rod tip and backed it off to the proper distance. A bullfrog clunked near the shore, to be answered by others farther on. There was a slight splash off to my left and I cast toward it with a buck-tailed wobbler, working in the lure slowly with gentle twitches of the rod tip. The lure caught solidly on a pad stem and we eased over to free it. Another splash resounded ahead of us, and I cast again.

This time, erupting spray flew where the lure landed and the quick jerk of the strike indicated that the bass was a big one. He ripped line from the spool as he stolidly wriggled for deeper water. I held the rod high in an effort to keep the line from catching on the pads and grasses.

"Better steer him to the left a bit," my host advised. "He'll work you into a mess where he's headed."

I changed direction of my rod, horsing him as much as I dared, and managed to turn him toward open water, my forefinger pressing against the reel spool to resist his taking out more line. He tried to go deep, but the same tactics brought him to the surface, where it seemed that his energetic splashing would flush every bass for a mile around. In open water eventually he gave in to firm handling on a tight line and soon docilely allowed me to lift him from his element and transfer him to the stringer.

We slid the canoe into a new position and started fishing again.

Several casts later, I dropped a lure toward the dim, protecting arms of a tree stump and connected solidly with a bass which seemed to have been waiting for the lure. Just then there was a splash behind me.

"Got one," I said.

"Got one, too," my companion chuckled.

Both fish were in open water, but their entanglement among the grasses near shore seemed imminent. With the approval of the other angler, I picked up a paddle with my left hand and sculled the canoe into deeper water.

"I'll wait till you get yours in," I advised. "Mine is not giving any trouble."

The brake and the anti-reverse mechanism of the reel held him on a tight line fifty feet or so from the canoe, where he swirled and gyrated in seeming contentment. The faint sheen of silver on the rippling blackness of the water indicated that there were no obstructions near him, so I let him maneuver about while I watched my companion land his prize — a bass obviously much bigger than mine.

Soon he netted him, and then I brought mine to boat. An hour later we totaled four large bass on the stringer and had released three more. Down the distant shore line, a beaconing speck of yellow light marked the location of our dock. The faded breeze had transformed the ripples of the lake into a glossy expanse of jet and the cooling air began to enshroud the stillness of the water with drifting streaks of fog. Even the frogs had stopped their bickering.

We secured our rods and slipped the paddles into the water, headed for home.

NIGHT FISHING FOR BASS

I have enjoyed night fishing with spinning tackle on many occasions both in fresh water and in salt but, fascinating though it is, I must say that I prefer being able to see what I am doing. If those who read this never have tried spinning in the dark, I hope they will do so; at least for a few times. When they do, the following comments may be helpful.

Picture Number 1 of "Casting Positions" shows that I prefer turning the pickup to the desired position by turning the reel's cup with the thumb and fingers of the reel hand. This, for the majority of fishermen, is easier under all circumstances than putting it in position by turning the reel's handle, but it is especially so at night because it can be done entirely by touch rather than by sight.

The occasional characteristic some reels have of allowing careless casts to half-hitch line around the pickup arm would be most annoying at night. Usually, I use reels with the pickup arm, but with the type of spool which prevents half-hitching, as described in Chapter Two. The bail-type reel is easy to use at night, and it would be almost impossible to get into difficulty with the manual type. Reels having spools which cover the cup also are an advantage in the dark, because they prevent loose line from becoming caught in the gears back of the spool.

Even in total blackness, one easily can become accustomed to handling the lure and to knowing by intuition exactly where it is. When one senses that it nearly is reeled in, the reeling should be done slowly enough so that one can feel it when the lure leaves the water. Another turn or two will raise it to the proper distance from the rod tip, this measurement guiding future retrieves.

In night fishing, we may get into trouble by failing to wind the line with constant tension on to the reel; especially when using surface lures such as popping plugs, where the combination of tight and loose reeling is hard to avoid. Feeling of the line with our fingers can tell us if its coils are loose or not; and, if they are, a cast to open water and proper reeling under tension will set things to rights again. Whenever the line becomes too loosely reeled, it should be respooled by this means, since casting with loose coils almost surely will lead into difficulty.

The chief advantage of braided nylon is that (usually being softer) it spools more evenly than monofilament when wound in under varying tension such as is apt to occur when fishing popping plugs and other floating lures. Anglers who have trouble spooling monofilament properly, in night fishing, may prefer the braided type for this reason. Also, these top water lures frequently are used near lily pads and other hazards where stronger-than-normal line for the tackle involved may be desired. If so, the softer braided nylon may be a good compromise, even though it may not be so desirable for other purposes.

A plug casting outfit compares even less favorably with spinning tackle by night than it does by day. I have been night fishing with several anglers addicted to plug-casting tackle and have noted that they spend more time muttering to themselves while picking out backlashes than they do in fishing. They usually have had to switch on a neck light to see well enough to remedy their difficulties and thus have spoiled fishing for others in the boat. One can get accustomed to seeing quite well in the dark if no lights are on, but the momentary glare of a light will ruin night vision for several minutes. Fortunately, however, the comparison between the two methods usually influences plug casters in favor of spinning gear when they go out again.

Spinning should not be considered as a man's sport alone. It is also an ideal method for women and children, since it is so easy for beginners to grasp its initial requirements.

Although my dear wife is as good a fly-fisher as the average of her sex, her more recent interest in spinning has contributed greatly to the mutual enjoyment of our days astream. In fact, I shall have to admit that I gave her her first spinning outfit partly in self-defense.

Our habit was to take our fly rods to one stream or another and for me to get her tackle put together and to settle her in a likely spot. She knew how to rig the gear herself, but she usually bowed to the edicts of chivalry in allowing me to do it, after excusing herself with a few "Oh, no, let me"s which did not sound overly convincing. Accoutered for the fray and with a goodly selection of flies, leaders and everything else she needed, I would give her suggestions on how to fish the water and admonish her to be careful with her backcasts.

Then, leaving her with a reasonable amount of water to herself, I would start manipulations at a discreet distance behind her. Since fishing always is better from the other side of the stream, I would wade the fast water and snake through the undergrowth to a likely run or riffle in which I thought there might be a goodly trout. With the family chores thus done, and properly "on location" myself, I would start to lay out a cast. And then —

"Joe-ee," would come a plaintive call from upriver. "Joe-ee, I'm afraid I'm hung up!"

"Break loose and put on a new fly," I would call back.

"Can't," she'd say. "But *please* don't bother to come back."

Quite obviously, if she hadn't wanted me to come back, she never would have called to me in the first place. So I would reel in the line, wriggle back through the bushes to where I could wade the river, complete the crossing, go upriver to the scene of the difficulty, get her rerigged — and we would start all over again. It was a cycle that went on and on.

So I bought her a spinning outfit.

Freed from troubles with backcasts, and with lures so much easier to tie on, she flipped her little offerings as expertly as anyone could wish for. Our piscatorial difficulties thus were ended — or practically so. We have had a lot more fun fishing together ever since.

Graduation for her came when we spent the night on a beach at Block Island spinning for bluefish. It was as dark as nights can get. I built a fire in the lee of a rock for her headquarters, but the bluefish were in the surf and she ignored the fire completely. She used the tackle most successfully all night long and only called for assistance once. I think she was hooked into a large sting ray at the time.

Her newly found independence with spinning tackle has inspired her to become equally independent with the fly rod. She rigs her own gear and, when the breeze carries her fly into a tree, she straightens out her difficulties alone. She's getting to be quite a lot of fun to go fishing with!

My young daughter at this point is a commendable disciple also. She takes to spinning as a duck takes to water. After observing her progress and that of others, it seems wise to me for parents to teach their youngsters to handle a spinning rod first and for them to learn the intricacies of fly fishing later. In their early stages, the spinning outfit produces fewer difficulties, and its amazing adaptability aids them in becoming more successful in their fishing; both attributes resulting in the initial encouragement needed so badly by young anglers. It helps them greatly if we can start them young, teach them correctly and provide them with properly chosen equipment.

The pleasures of angling are a priceless heritage endowed by the lore of the ages. Spinning, perhaps the youngest of angling methods, now vies with all others in popularity. Although its growing pains are subsiding, we shall for some time need to use discrimination in selecting appropriate tackle and in accepting advice on how best to use it. I hope that this book proves to be a helpful step in this direction. I shall be most happy if it brings to all who read it as many fascinating days astream as spinning has brought to me.

Postscript

Spinning for
Salt Water Game Fish

DURING THE YEARS since *Spinning for American Game Fish* was published in 1947, the sport has come of age in America. As this, its successor, is written, a lot more and a lot better tackle has become available — and we now know a great deal more about how to use it. Most of the scoffers who habitually decry innovations of all sorts have stopped scoffing, and even the dyed-in-the-wool "purists" have come to admit that spinning is one of the most useful and most sporting of all angling methods, if the tackle is used in the manner for which it was intended.

To enable us to enjoy spinning to the utmost, the power of the tackle must be in proportion to the power of the fish. We have baby reels, delicate rods, gossamer lines and miniature lures for small fish, and we can have a lot of fun with this diminutive equipment even for much bigger ones. We have stronger gear for more powerful adversaries, even including equipment equal to the largest surface fighters found in the ocean.

The late Arthur Williams, noted book designer for Little, Brown and Company, at my suggestion took a spinning outfit to Mazatlan, on Mexico's western coast, to try to catch a big sailfish or marlin on the lightest equipment so far used. With a Ru Mer spinning reel and eight-pound-test nylon monofilament line, he brought three times to boat a black marlin reliably estimated to weigh over a hundred and fifty pounds! The angler enabled the native boatman to grasp the leader wire each time but, in the rough water, the fish was lost in landing. This is one of several instances which prove the amazing adaptability of spinning gear for taking game fish of every size with the lightest and sportiest tackle imaginable.

As this is written, salt water spinning still is in a developmental stage, but its suitability for taking big game fish has been proved thousands of times over. Up and down both coasts, wherever breakers roll or tidal waters extend inland, salt water fishermen are neglecting their customary gear because of their preference for spinning.

Some of us have been experimenting with the spinning method in salt water for several years. Sailfish, school tuna, bonefish, yellowtail, albacore, tarpon, snook, channel bass, striped bass, bluefish, dolphin and others too numerous to mention have fallen to the rods of spinning anglers and, with this tackle, official world's records are being broken.

I am one of the first to admit that we have a lot to learn about salt water spinning, but so much already has been learned that it seems proper to place this knowledge at the disposal of anglers who are lucky enough to be able to go fishing in salt water. There, only the elements dictate the closed season. There, we have valiant game fish in abundance, including bigger ones than have yet been caught.

Consequently, a companion volume, *Spinning for Salt Water Game Fish,* is being prepared for publication in the near future. While the fresh water tackle which has been described here may be used for many of the smaller species, larger fish often require something a bit sturdier. A great deal of the tackle and a great many of the tactics are so different that an individual specialized book has seemed appropriate. I trust that *Spinning for Salt Water Game Fish* will prove helpful to other anglers and I hope that those who are so fortunate as to enjoy the bounties of Father Neptune's domain will gain as much pleasure and profit from salt water spinning as the sport has brought to me.